Backtracking

Backtracking

By Foot,

Canoe,

and Subaru

└ Along the Lewis and Clark Trail

Benjamin Long

Photographs by Karen Nichols

SASQUATCH
BOOKS
SEATTLE

For my mother, who took me to the library,
and my father, who took me to the mountains.

Text copyright ©2000 by Benjamin Long
Photographs copyright ©2000 by Karen Nichols

Published by Sasquatch Books
Distributed in Canada by Raincoast Books Ltd.
Printed in the United States of America

05 04 03 02 01 00   5 4 3 2 1

Cover and interior design: Karen Schober
Cover photographs: Top (Missouri River) © Karen Nichols; right (White Water Canoeing Slalom Race) © Richard Hamilton Smith/CORBIS; left (Prairie Dog) © RaymondGehman/CORBIS.
Map illustration: Karen Schober
Interior composition: Dan McComb
Copy editor: Don Graydon

Library of Congress Cataloging in Publication Data
Long, Benjamin.
    Backtracking by foot, canoe, and Subaru along the Lewis and Clark Trail / Benjamin Long.
       p.   cm.
    Includes bibliographical references and index.
    ISBN 1-57061-246-3 (alk. paper)
    I. Lewis and Clark National Historic Trail—Description and travel. 2. West (U.S.)—
Description and travel. 3. Natural history—Lewis and Clark National Historic Trail. 4.
Natural history—West (U.S.) 5. Long, Benjamin—Journeys—West (U.S.) 6. Lewis and Clark
Expedition (1804-1806) I. Title: Backtracking. II. Title.
F592.7.L84 2000   00-024107
917.804'34—dc21

SASQUATCH BOOKS
615 Second Avenue
Seattle, Washington 98104
(206) 467-4300
www.SasquatchBooks.com
books@SasquatchBooks.com

America stretched out like a buffalo skin,
aerial and clear night of the gallop,
there toward the starry heights
I drink your glass of green dew.

—Pablo Neruda, *Canto General*

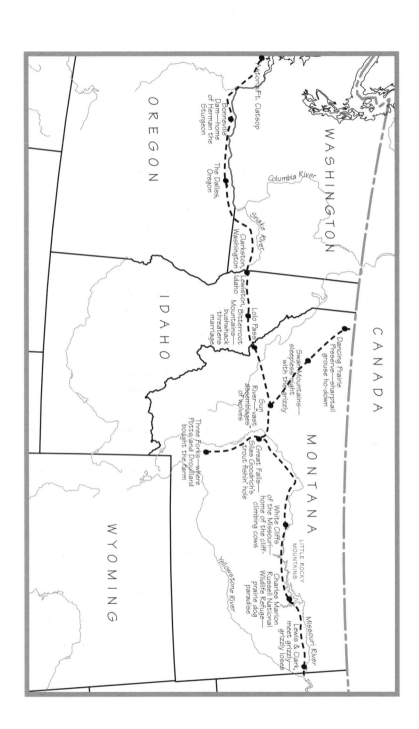

Astoria/Ft. Clatsop

Bonneville
Dam—home
of Herman the
Sturgeon

O R E G O N

The Dalles,
Oregon

Columbia River

W A S H I N G T O N

Snake River

Clarkston, Washington

Lewiston, Idaho

Bitterroot
Mountains—
bushwhack
threatens
marriage

Lolo Pass

I D A H O

Swan Mountains—
sleepless night
with the grizzly

Dancing Prairie
Preserve—sharptail
grouse ho-down

Sun
River—"vast
assemblages"
of wolves

C A N A D A

Three Forks—where
Potts and Drouillard
bought the farm

Great Falls—
Silas Goodrich's
trout fishin' hole

M O N T A N A

White Cliffs
of the Missouri—
home of the cliff-
climbing cows

W Y O M I N G

Yellowstone River

LITTLE ROCKY
MOUNTAINS

Charles Marion
Russell National
Wildlife Refuge—
prairie dog
paradise

Missouri River

Lewis & Clark
meet grizzly,
grizzly loses

Contents

Chapter 1

Reasonable and Prudent

AN INTRODUCTION

SOMETIMES IN MONTANA, IT SNOWS IN AUGUST.
You fall asleep to thunder and awake to white silence. And not just in the mountains. Even on the valley floor, where the towns and farms are, a summer snow can stick for days. Although it shatters the

fruit trees and leaves the barn swallows dead on their mud-cup nests, the freak precipitation somehow sanctifies the landscape, as fresh snow always does. The land is suddenly a new, unstained place. A blank map. It is an illusion, but summer snow can make you believe you are walking where no one has stepped before. Exploring. On these rare days, I stop whatever I am doing and go tracking.

I used to track with my hunter's heart—pursuing whatever creature laid down the sign. Trying to run it down. I hungered for even a glimpse of it. It might be a moose or a weasel or anything. If I caught sight of the creature, even just the animal crashing away in a shattered second, it made my heart beat faster. It was Michael Fairchild who taught me another way. The way of back-tracking.

When I met him, Mike was a wolfer. In those days, big gray, black, and white wolves were creeping out of Canada into Montana. These were the first wolves to hunt the West in fifty years. Mike was waiting for them. He buried No. 4 Newhouse traps along the packs' runways and sprinkled granular snow over the traps' patient jaws. He was not trapping for pelts or vengeance. He was a scientist, trapping for knowledge. Mike would capture wolves, tranquilize them, place radio collars around their necks, and let them go. Just one or two wolves per pack, so he might learn from them. He checked his traps each morning, so the wolves wouldn't hurt themselves in capture. If he caught a wolf on a particularly cold day, he would cup the trapped paw of the anesthetized wolf in his bare hands to warm it. He would hold the paw until he was certain the wolf's circulation had returned and the animal could run again.

The wolves ran in rugged, mountainous country where the terrain frequently blocked or misdirected signals from the radio collars. So Mike also had to backtrack the wolves. He would unravel their trails backward, traveling on foot, wearing cross-country skis or stubby little snowshoes. He backtracked the wolves over snowbound ridges, through the thickets, and across icy rivers. This way he learned their secrets.

Mike would notice the tiniest fleck of blood between the toes of a cougar print and follow the trail back to a partially eaten whitetail doe, cached under a scratching of pine needles. In a glance, he noted the difference between the trail of a common pine marten and that of a rare fisher. He showed me the otter slides along the creek banks and the feather marks where a goshawk missed a ruffed grouse and brushed empty snow. Mike was lithe as a cross-country ski and could turn gracefully on them, even when penetrating thickets of dogwood and willow. Sometimes, floundering behind him, I would grow impatient with his backtracking. The animals took us in illogical directions, through tangles and rock fields. There was always a known, seemingly logical route wherever we wanted to go, but these meanderings took us all around it. Mike's method took us farther away from my target, farther from what I believed was the prize.

"But this is the way you learn the truth," he told me. "If you follow, the animal is just reacting to your presence, trying to avoid you. Backtracking, you study the evidence as the animal laid it down."

"Yes," I said. "I understand that. But sometimes I like to see with my own eyes."

◆

FULLY LOADED, our Subaru had a certain Joad family look to it. *Grapes of Wrath* meets *Outside* magazine. Karen slammed the hatch, shutting the door on most of our possessions. Slamming it on our past lives.

The rearview mirror on the windshield reflected a mound of gear where the rear view used to be. Grub boxes stuffed with groceries and cookware. Coolers that sloshed with melting ice. Clinking bottles of white gas. Duffel bags of clothing to suit any weather; one tent and two sleeping bags; backpacks and hiking boots; a crate of cheap crankcase oil. Toolbox. Tackle box. Binoculars. Life jackets and canoe paddles. Karen's camera bags and my notebooks. Two mountain bikes hung over the hatchback. Our Mad River canoe was lashed belly-up to the roof rack. The bow protruded over the front of the car, so it took both of us to check the oil: I propped up the hood while Karen extracted the dipstick.

That summer, our home state of Montana had no highway speed limit. That is, there was no magic number, like fifty-five or sixty-five miles per hour, beyond which one was not allowed not drive. The law said only that one must drive in a "reasonable and prudent" manner.

The Subaru is not fast. Even new, the four-cylinder engine crammed sideways under the hood provided only adequate power. Now with 150,000 miles on it and pulling this load, the engine protested at highway speeds. One noise was grating and unnerving. The second was downright hideous. We named our enemies. The constant clatter of piston lifters was Roxy. When Roxy came to visit, we turned up the volume on the tape deck and tried to ignore her. Another, undiagnosed sound was Roxy's ugly cousin Helga. Helga sounded like a garbage disposal trying to devour a spoon. When Helga showed up, we worried about impending breakdowns and grew nervous and short-tempered. Sometimes Helga could be hushed with a quart of 10W-30. Sometimes not.

Karen blew her bangs from her eyes and tucked an errant curl behind an ear. She shook her head and looked at me. I smiled and shrugged. We had discussed this moment a thousand times. We had counted up our savings, worked through the budgets. We had voiced our dreams and shed our tears. There was not much more to say. This was the time to act.

Karen and I are the results of two different cultures. Karen is from "back East." I am from "out West." By some lucky piece of geometry, we met in Montana. It's a tricky business, reducing a complex, physical, beautiful person to ink. Especially when the person is your wife. Karen is a lover of life and of people and an appreciator of beauty. As such, she is also a photographer.

Karen absorbs light, as if she could synthesize the stuff into her life's energy. She has taught me to sit on a mountain slope above timberline and spend the entire afternoon watching light shift, taking in the cloud shadows racing across the sky and the slant of the sun basking every face and crevice on the mountain in an ever-changing glow. Some nights when she dreams, she holds one hand in front of her face and pushes an imaginary shutter release, and I wonder what mystical scenes her mind's eye wishes to record.

So the two of us stood there. We were four years deep into our marriage. We sold our house, extracting ourselves from the thirty-year mortgage. We quit the jobs we had held for a combined fifteen years. We liquidated our possessions in a bloodletting procession of garage sales. There was no going back.

As we crated our last possessions, stacking boxes in a friend's basement, I found myself excited but anxious. At night in our empty house, I stared awake for hours hoping the ceiling would tell me we weren't making some monumental mistake.

Karen and I had fallen in love on a mountaintop. We had fallen in love on a river. We knew those places were where we were at our best, both for ourselves and for each other. Our first Valentine's night together was spent in a tepee on an alpine ridgetop, with the thermometer reading twenty below zero and the wind whipping at thirty miles per hour. When the dawn broke cold and still, the entire world seemed clear.

Now, we were weary of careers that found us impounded in our cubicles. So I recruited Karen to follow a dream. It was a dream that germinated in a boy's mind, and continued to grow and take root during youth. The dream was pruned and chopped back during adulthood but refused to keep to its place. It was a dream with a will of its own. The most dangerous kind.

We wanted out. If only for a while. If only for once in our lives, we wanted to see our world unfiltered. We wanted to see what we would find, both in the world beyond and the world within. When it was time to go, we didn't even lock the house. Instead, I handed the keys to the new owners, shook their hands and wished them luck. They returned the wish, shaking our hands as if we needed more luck than they did. I backed out of the driveway and smacked into their new sedan. Their fender crumpled. Crumbs of taillight decorated the asphalt.

"*Shit*," I said. "If we were reasonable and prudent, we would never leave the driveway."

◆

WHERE DID THIS START, this idea of the Great American Road Trip? Tracing the idea back to its source, I tripped up on the Lewis and Clark Expedition.

The journals of Lewis and Clark. Mark Twain's stagecoach in *Roughing It.* The Joads' jalopy in *Grapes of Wrath.* Jack Kerouac hitchhiking in *On the Road;* John Wayne's horse in *Stagecoach* to Susan Sarandon's convertible in *Thelma and Louise.* All of them follow the idea—if not the exact route—that was branded into the American imagination by Lewis and Clark's Voyage of Discovery. That is, Americans push westward. When the East gets too crowded, too impoverished, too stiff, too dull, too oppressive, Americans strike off into the western wilderness. For two hundred years, the West has promised wealth, escape, wonder, adventure, as sure as the first official explorers for the United States, Lewis and Clark, found herds of bison and free-flowing rivers. No matter the problem Americans shouted into the wind, the answer echoed back: Run West.

It's not just in storybooks or Hollywood cinema. Most of my friends come from back East. My parents are transplants from east of the one hundredth meridian. Karen grew up within earshot of the Washington, D.C., Beltway. Problem is, some of us were *born* in the West. Where were we to run?

When I was a kid in history class, Lewis and Clark was required reading every year. My junior high was just north of the Lewis and Clark Trail, the Clearwater River flowing to the south of us. Just as our soccer team took on the squad from Sacagawea Junior High every season, our history book took on the Northwest Passage, the Louisiana Purchase, and the Corps of Discovery. The pages, usually dry as chalk dust, somehow came alive.

We followed the Corps's laden keelboat as they launched up the Missouri River near St. Louis. We waited out their first frigid winter in the Mandan village of North Dakota. We followed the crew through the gauntlet of grizzly bears and waterfalls, up the Missouri and across Montana. We learned of Sacagawea's tearful reunion with her brother, Chief Cameahwait, in the Lemhi Mountains. We stepped in the Corps's soggy moccasin tracks across the starvation snows of the Lolo Trail.

We read of their near-poisoning by the salmon-and-camas diet of the Nez Perce. We followed their dugout pine logs down the Clearwater and Snake, and through the mighty rapids of the Columbia. We read, over and over again, "Ocian in view!" as they approached the Pacific. We skimmed over the rain-soaked drudgery of Fort Clatsop. (Or Fort Catsup, as we kids called it.)

We retraced the Corps's anticlimactic but perilous rush home, grunting back over the Lolo Trail. We knew the dynamic duo split up back in Montana, Clark canoeing down the Yellowstone River, Lewis getting into Indian trouble up near Canada. They rejoined then, in the midst of that great empty plain, and sailed to a hero's welcome in St. Louis.

I grew up on a fork of the Palouse River, which Lewis had called Drewyer's River in honor of the expedition's master hunter, George Drouillard. My neighborhood friends nailed together "canoes" of two-by-fours and plywood. We portaged them through the long river grass, planning to float downstream as far as the muddy creek would carry us. Our craft promptly sank to the muddy bottom of the Drewyer's. We were home for supper.

Undaunted, we returned to our imaginary trek. An old pickup deserted in a vacant lot became a keelboat to pull up an imaginary Missouri River. Our bicycles were war ponies gained from the

Shoshone. The groundskeeper chasing us off the municipal golf course was a Blackfeet warrior hot for our scalps. I wanted to name my Labrador retriever puppy *Seaman,* after Lewis's dog. My parents, for reasons they would not explain, refused to allow it. Of all the passages from the journals of Lewis and Clark, the ones that fueled my imagination-fire were those with images of wilderness and wildlife.

THE VOYAGE OF DISCOVERY was the first exploratory expedition sponsored by the United States of America. It was the first link in a chain of exploration that put men on the moon, robots on Mars, and telescopes probing beyond the bounds of our galaxy. The trek took place when the tree of western science was a sapling, biology its initial branch. Carl Linnaeus, creator of binomial nomenclature, died twenty-five years before the expedition. Charles Darwin, who would introduce rudimentary concepts of evolution, was born three years after its return. In the era of Lewis and Clark, scientists were still battling the myth of spontaneous generation—the widely held idea that maggots simply sprouted from rotten meat, and tadpoles emerged unbidden from mud.

Lewis and Clark were first soldiers, not scientists. But their boss, Thomas Jefferson, was probably the most scientifically minded president the United States has ever elected. He turned both captains into scientist-soldiers. According to historians who specialize in these things, Lewis and Clark discovered some 122 varieties of animals and 178 types of plants on their march west. (I hesitate to call them *discoveries,* since every creature and plant was intimately known to the native people Lewis and Clark met on their path, and often known to French, English, and Spanish trappers and soldiers as well.)

In essence, the expedition was an eight-thousand-mile experiment—a test of the hypothesis that North America could be crossed by water, that the fabled Northwest Passage existed. The experiment succeeded, even if the hypothesis was disproved. On the way, members of the Corps of Discovery stumbled upon some three hundred species or subspecies that no one in their culture had ever recorded. Towering ponderosa pines with thick, corky bark. The Clarkia, a delicate purple flower with petals shaped like moose antlers. Fleeting pronghorn antelope that ran with the grace of flying birds. The western tanager, with feathers the colors of tropical flowers. On average, once every third day of their twenty-eight-month journey the explorers ran across something new. When one reviews these journals and add imagination to the sketchy physical evidence, the findings are not just discoveries. They become stories.

Take, for example, a small botanical discovery that came from one of Lewis's greatest blunders of the expedition, during the return trip to St. Louis. In late July 1806, Lewis and three crew members split off from the main expedition. They wandered north, to explore the Rocky Mountain Front in what is now Montana. The small patrol marched into the high plains toward the headwaters of the Marias River. A generation after the Revolutionary War, Lewis wanted to see if this stream drained property claimed by England.

Moreover, Lewis led his men deep into the territory of the Blackfeet. Lewis had not met these proud, bison-hunting nomads, but knew their fearsome reputation. Lewis assumed them to be hostile toward the Americans. In the Two Medicine River drainage, they met a small band of this tribe. The Blackfeet rode muscular, adorned horses and were armed with strong, stubby bows and cast-off guns obtained from British traders. The explorers shared a pipe with the natives and camped along with them, but slept with a guard on post.

According to Lewis's side of the story, he awoke at dawn to find several young warriors attempting to steal horses and guns. A brief fight ensued. An explorer stabbed a Blackfeet warrior through the heart, and the warrior crumpled dead. Lewis pursued the others with his rifle, shooting one Indian in the stomach. The wounded tribesman returned fire, and Lewis heard the rifle ball zing past his ear.

As suddenly as the fight began, it was over. Lewis found his men isolated on the plain, vastly outnumbered and far from any backup. He measured the depth of his tactical error and took the only logical recourse: He gathered the remaining horses and ran like hell. His little squad galloped across the prairie. They sped toward the Missouri River, to the point where they planned to rendezvous with the remainder of the Corps. They were riding for their lives. They could not have held off a full attack by the Blackfeet. All one day and into the next, their horses' hooves pounded the prairie sod.

Suddenly, in the midst of this flight, Lewis reined his horse to a stop. He dismounted and bent to the ground. From the corner of his eye, he had spotted a plant he did not recognize. He took a sample. It was later named white-margined spurge. *Euphorbia marginata.* Nothing fancy. But a plant new to science.

◆

SUCH STORIES INTRIGUED ME. Stories of the American wilderness, and these people—for better or worse, my people—trying to come to grips with it. I was intrigued by rivers where an axman could fell a pine tree, burn out the heartwood, and paddle downstream to the ocean. I could only imagine a winter prairie, the frigid air fogged with the breath of ten thousand buffalo. I pictured steelhead leaping through the mist of Celilo Falls on the Columbia and the bright lung blood coughed up by a wounded grizzly, running headlong into bullets in one valiant final charge.

As a boy, I believed—believed not only in my imagination but in my heart—that I could somehow escape to that world. I believed that somewhere, beyond the schoolyard, beyond the boundaries of our town, beyond the mountains on the edge of town, that such places and creatures still existed. Surely somewhere in the modern American West, fragments of that aboriginal wilderness remained.

Now, after all these years, the dream had taken hold once more. This was where Karen and I were headed: to search out fragments of America's primal wildness. It would not be a direct route. This would require some backtracking.

Chapter 2

A Precious Pestilence

BLACK-TAILED PRAIRIE DOG
Cynomys ludovicianus

ONLY THE NAME OF THIS HIGH-PLAINS TOWN—MALTA—
and perhaps the ferocious sunlight,
reminded me of anything remotely
Mediterranean. Everything else was
straight Montana. Grain elevators. Brick
school. Cowboy bar. The surrounding

plains, flat as the bottom of an ocean. After all, that's what they are—the bottom of an ancient seaway that covered the Great Plains under leagues of saltwater. Later, these plains supported short-grass prairie and unfathomable herds of bison. Today they grow wheat for two dollars a bushel. The fields are plowed in alternating strips, running north-south to the horizon. One strip is last season's stubble, the next strip is this year's furrows. This pattern discourages wind erosion and reflects a harsh lesson taught by the dust bowl of the 1930s. In these broad bands of alternating earth tones, the land looks like it's wearing a giant rugby jersey.

When Karen and I arrived in Malta, the thermometer at the downtown bank read 100 even. The headline across the *Billings Gazette* was four bold letters: HEAT. We camped outside town in a muggy cottonwood grove along the Milk River, a stream named by Meriwether Lewis because its color reminded him of the distant luxury of milk and tea. We pitched our tent beside a train trestle that we thought picturesque. At dusk, we realized the track was the Hi Line, the busiest rail route across the northern tier states, by which Burlington Northern locomotives rumble the breadth of the Great Plains. The route connects the farms and cities of the Midwest to the ports of Puget Sound.

Rail traffic was brisk. The trains were regular and fully nocturnal. At each passing, the earth trembled through the floor of the tent and the train sounded as if it would jump track and plow us over. During the only lull in the night's rail traffic, the county's mosquito abatement truck swept through. We jolted awake to the manic yellow roof light and the racket of a generator-powered pump. The rig fogged the night in a noxious mist. The night dragged against our fight for sleep. The instant the sun breached the eastern horizon, our little nylon greenhouse grew unbearably hot. We squeezed our eyes shut and sprawled atop the sleeping bags, pleading with the gods of sleep for a few moments of rest. Our sweaty skin stuck to the nylon, and sleep was impossible.

With that, we abandoned camp for town. We parked in a faded slot downtown and entered a cafe for coffee and a paper. After breakfast, we found a laundromat and a grocery store. The store was air-conditioned, so we dawdled there while our clothes spun, picking through the selection of wilted produce, stocking up with block ice for the cooler. The clerk wore that too-bored-to-stand look favored by adolescents everywhere. She took our out-of-town check without hesitation.

"What brings you to Malta?" she said.

It seemed foolish to tell her the truth: prairie dogs. We had driven across the prairie in sweltering heat and spent a sleepless night tormented by freight trains and malathion in order to watch rodents. Rodents that most local people think of as pests, if they think of them at all. So Karen said we were here to meet Randy Matchett, a U.S. Fish and Wildlife Service biologist who is a member of a team trying to rescue black-footed ferrets. The ferrets are arguably the most critically endangered mammal on the continent. That was also a true answer and sounded more respectable.

"Oh, the ferrets," the clerk said. "Those expensive coyote snacks."

We had arrived in Malta a couple days ahead of schedule. We had been canoeing on the Missouri River, but heat exhaustion and mosquitoes had driven us back to land. Downstream from here, the Lewis and Clark Trail on the Missouri River is flooded beneath the waters of Fort Peck Reservoir. We had hoped to enjoy the Great Plains before meeting Matchett. Only with this heat, there was no thought of enjoying the plains. Only the thought of escaping them. We drove south on U.S. Highway 191, crossing the plains at a reasonable-and-prudent eighty miles per hour. We drove toward an isolated range of low mountains called the Little Rockies. These were the first mountains spied by the Corps of Discovery.

After the explorers spent much of 1804 pulling their boats up the Missouri River, they built Fort Mandan in what is now North Dakota. There they hunkered down and waited out winter temperatures of -43°F. At Fort Mandan, the expedition picked up Sacagawea and there she gave birth to Jean Baptiste.

With spring of 1805, the Corps struck out again, as the Missouri River curved to the west. They marched across what is now North Dakota, past the mouth of another great western river, the Yellowstone, and then past the Milk. One May morning in 1805, Clark climbed above the bluffs of the Missouri for a look-see. He scanned the horizon with his spyglass and saw this mountain range in the distance. Clark believed the Little Rockies to be the mountains, or at least similar to the mountains, his crew would have to cross from the Missouri to the Columbia drainage.

Clark was sorely mistaken. In fact, the Little Rockies are an island range—a small, isolated mound bobbing from the plains like a stone ship rising above a rolling ocean. One could walk around them without ever gaining elevation. From their pine-covered ridges, one can look across the sweep of the flatlands, to other distant ranges noted by the Corps and that others later named: the Highwoods, the Judiths. To the east is the Bear's Paw Range and the Fort Belknap Indian Reservation.

Looking at a map of this country, one notes that the Fort Belknap Reservation is nearly a perfect square, except for the conspicuously missing southeast corner. A cake with one piece removed. The Little Rockies, by all cartographic logic, should fill that corner. And they would have, too, except for the fact the Little Rockies contained gold. The Little Rockies were prospected by pick and shovel a century ago and omitted from reservation boundaries.

Today it takes not only faith to move mountains, but also investment capital. Since the 1960s, the Little Rockies have been shaved flat and hollowed out in pursuit of gold. A few hundred people were employed for a spell, while a few investors pulled in big returns when gold prices were high. But markets shift. In the 1990's bull market, conservative investments like precious metals fell out of favor. Ore prices dropped and the mine shut down. No matter the rehabilitation, the efforts will never return the range to the profile that greeted Clark's spyglass.

Karen and I aimed the Subaru for the Little Rockies, seeking relief through altitude. Perhaps we would find shade and running water. At the least, we wanted to escape the jurisdiction of the mosquito abatement truck. We drove south across Phillips County. The distances here are as broad as any in the United States, except those on the tundra of Alaska. The span of the landscape takes on mystical dimension, as if one were a Borges character crossing Las Pampas of Argentina. My foot weighed heavy on the accelerator.

The highway was flanked by fences. The posts were not proper posts at all, but a hodgepodge of brittle sticks, all crooked and cut to different lengths and connected by three strands of barbed wire. The posts were not driven into the hard pan, and the fence was held in place by its own tension, like a bad marriage. Behind the fences stood Angus cattle, which appeared capable of flattening them at whim.

Every twenty miles or so, a dirt road ran perpendicular to the highway, disappearing into the horizon. Driveways. One weathered mailbox standing guard. Only rarely was a ranch house in view. When a home was visible, there was likely as not a roping dummy in the yard: a fiberglass steer head affixed to a straw bale. In the plains, roping dummies in the yards are as common as basketball hoops over suburban garage doors. Phillips County is home to roughly five thousand people and seventy-seven thousand cattle. Angus, mostly, but also Herefords and a few Charolais. Cows. Cows. Cows. When Karen and I stopped for lemonade in one Phillips County restaurant, the menu offered six dinner specials. All were steak.

Yet even here, cattle are spaced almost as widely as the people. The aridity of the place demands it. Cows, like people, must drink. That, it occurs to me, is the miracle of the prairie dog.

One cannot fully appreciate this miracle until you've visited the Great Plains under the full weight of summer. Light beats at your cranium like a ball peen hammer. The light is incessant, from the first crack of dawn until the enemy orb finally retreats to the west. Lark buntings and vesper sparrows perch on the barbed wire, holding their wings away from their bodies, their beaks agape, trying to shed the inescapable heat. Mammals—humans for instance—demand water. Anything wet. A trickle for the throat. A stock tank to dunk in. If not water, then shade. A body pleads for it. And the mute plain offers neither. Just another heaping serving of sun.

Animals demand water. Except for the prairie dogs. They can make do without liquid water, as do some Saharan species of gerbil. They're fine, thanks, with the crisp stalks of native grass. No water today. None tomorrow. None until the end of the drought. They can do this for years, if need be. This phenomenon was first observed by one Meriwether Lewis.

There is no saying exactly how many prairie dogs inhabited the Great Plains when the Corps of Discovery crossed it. "Innumerable" was the figure the captains settled on in their journals. Modern scientists estimate "innumerable" was perhaps five billion, give or take a billion. Prairie dogs were ubiquitous on short-grass prairie, which covered a fifth of North America. Prairie dogs far outnumbered the storied herds of bison and elk. They were roughly as numerous as passenger pigeons.

In September 1804, the Corps of Discovery found the land near Boyd County, Nebraska, pockmarked with thousands of burrows. Members of the Corps were both charmed and puzzled by the rodent. Lewis compared the bark of the animal to the yapping of the lapdogs popular in fashionable Virginia. But evidently Sgt. John Ordway coined the term *prairie dog*. On days when the Corps did not have luck hunting bison or elk, the men potted prairie dogs instead. After all, these were backwoods boys from Kentucky and Virginia, raised on squirrel. "This little animal is frequently very fat and its flesh is not unpleasant," wrote Lewis. He later described prairie dog meat as "well flavored and tender."

The captains walked across prairie-dog towns several miles across. Individual dog towns were megalopolitan affairs, containing millions of rodents and stretching over hundreds of square miles. Burrows offer not only shelter from the sun, but also from most avian and terrestrial predators. The rodents tunnel through hard-packed soil, digging underground homes complete with latrines, nursing and sleeping quarters, and listening chambers near both the front and back doors. The animals pile dirt at the entrances of a burrow until the entrances look like miniature craters. The design helps prevent the burrow from flooding during spring rain squalls and also serves to improve ventilation underground. By raising the one entrance a few inches above the other, prairie dogs manipulate air pressure in the burrow, providing a steady flow of air and preventing stagnation that would otherwise render the burrow uninhabitable.

The Corps was under standing orders to closely observe all living novelties. So the men spent nearly a full September day in 1804 trying to capture a prairie dog alive. They attacked the burrows with shovels, eventually discovering the rodents were the better diggers. Then, with two men left guarding the boats, the Corps took to flooding the burrows, carrying barrel after barrel of Missouri River water across the prairie to pour into the earth. "Caught one alive by poreing a great quantity of water down his hole," Clark later wrote. The creature was caged and put aboard a boat.

In subsequent days the Corps's floating menagerie added a sharptail grouse and a few magpies, all creatures previously unknown to science. These animals were kept alive through the winter at Fort Mandan. In spring, the ice broke from the Missouri River and Lewis sent a keelboat back to civilization. He loaded the craft with journals and letters, coyote bones, Mandan weaponry, fossils of a prehistoric sea creature, the magpies and the prairie dog, and other trophies. He sent the works back to President Jefferson. The keelboat's cargo passed through the hands of various traders, boatmen, and longshoremen. The keelboat floated sixteen hundred miles down the Missouri from Fort Mandan to St. Louis. From there, the cargo was taken another one thousand miles down the Mississippi to New Orleans. At New Orleans, the crates and cages were loaded on a sailboat, which traveled around the tip of Florida and up the southern seaboard. After four months, the ship crossed to Chesapeake Bay, near Baltimore. Only a day's journey from Washington, D.C., where Jefferson waited, the boat hit rough water. The ship lost a substantial portion of cargo in the storm, but the prairie dog and one of the magpies survived. The magpie died shortly after its arrival. But the prairie dog lived out its days in a Philadelphia museum, having traveled some four thousand miles.

It was during the prairie dog's captivity at Fort Mandan that Lewis made a remarkable discovery. "I am astonished at how this anamal exists as it dose without water," Lewis wrote. The thing didn't drink.

Early naturalists hypothesized that the rodents lived on dew or burrowed down to groundwater. But later scientists demonstrated that captive prairie dogs could survive for years without liquid water. Their secret is a super-efficient pair of kidneys, which allow the animals to use and reuse water gleaned from the grasses and forbs that make up their diet.

Humans, on the other hand, are not so superbly adapted to arid climates. We seek the shade of an aspen stand and a six-pack cooled in a mountain stream. Karen and I found that in the Little Rockies. We slept a day away, far from the ruckus of the railroad and the mosquito abatement crew.

WHEN IN NEW COUNTRY, Karen and I tend to seek out birds. Birds offer insightful introduction to a place, from landscape to microsite. Prairie-dog towns are no exception. There are birds to be found among prairie dogs that you are unlikely to find any-place else. The ecologists' cliche is that prairie dog towns are the supermarkets of the prairie. Prairie dogs themselves are the stock on the shelves, attracting predators from bobcats to golden eagles. Safety in numbers is the oldest adage. Prairie dogs know this well. When an eagle's shadow skims over a dog town, the rodents give a whistle and scurry for cover. Aside from eagles, prairie dogs attract ferruginous hawks, *Buteo regalis,* which translates to the "regal hawk." Ferruginous hawks were probably the most common raptor to fly over the Corps of Discovery on the plains. But in the past two hundred years, they have been largely displaced by Swainson's and red-tailed hawks. Ferruginous hawks prefer vast, unbroken prairie. Swainson's hawks and red-tails are more compatible with today's cultivated fields, telephone poles, and shelter belts.

The burrowing owl is a small, scowling bird with a face that looks like it holds a grudge against the world. It does not dig burrows itself, but takes claim of deserted prairie-dog holes. The owl can be seen standing guard at the burrow's edge. If it sees trouble coming, the owl drops inside and buzzes a remarkable mimic of a rattlesnake. Nosy predators move on. This close relationship between owls and prairie dogs is sometimes problematic for owls. They are commonly killed alongside their hosts during rodent control campaigns. I once saw an owl that had been gassed in one such campaign; its eyeballs rolled in their sockets like chestnuts loose in their shells.

The mountain plover likewise depends on prairie-dog colonies. The plovers pick insects out of the close-cropped grass and evade their enemies by freezing utterly still. Their coats are patterned like the dirty, trimmed grass of the dog town. The mountain plover is dangerously near extinction, mostly because of the eradication of prairie-dog towns.

So Karen and I packed our battered field guides and binoculars, filled our water jugs, and left the cool shelter of our mountain camp. We drove toward the Charles M. Russell National Wildlife Refuge—a million-acre preserve named for cowboy artist Charles Marion Russell, who so often portrayed this landscape on canvas. As evening arrived, Karen and I drove into the prairie and the rich light. It felt as if we were driving into one of Charlie's paintings, looking for a prairie-dog town.

When it comes to cataloging wildlife, biologists tend to be lumpers or splitters. Lumpers consider prairie dogs to include only two species: black-tailed and white-tailed. Splitters divide them into five species. Based on more subtle differences in geography and biology, they add species they call the Mexican, Gunnison, and Utah. We sought the black-tailed prairie dog, the most widespread variety and the form the Corps encountered in 1804. Historically the black-tailed prairie dog could be found across the breadth of the central United States, from southern Canada to northern Mexico.

Unlike most rodents, black-tailed prairie dogs remain active in the harshest of seasons, neither hibernating during the bitter cold of winter nor sleeping through the dry months of summer. Black-tailed prairie dogs are social creatures, living in family groups called coteries. Scientists have deciphered eleven distinct chirps from black-tailed dogs. Some believe, for example, that there is one chirp to warn against an incoming eagle, another for a stalking bobcat. The football-size rodents look a little like overfed kindergarten gerbils. They have the endearing habit of greeting each other with kisses. On the other hand, they occasionally practice cannibalism.

Black-tailed prairie dogs once occupied an estimated 100 million to 250 million acres in North America, mostly in sprawling, interlinked colonies. As we have plowed and poisoned the plains, we have cut that to less than 1 million acres, perhaps as little as

700,000, scattered in isolated fragments across 10 large states. Where there were once perhaps 5 billion prairie dogs, there are now as few as 7 million. The destruction of prairie-dog habitat represents a greater ecological change than, for example, the logging of old-growth forest in the Pacific Northwest. When one gauges the percentage of habitat destroyed or the percentage of the population exterminated, the black-tailed prairie dog has suffered more than the grizzly bear under the industrialization of the West.

Of course there are a lot more individual prairie dogs than there are individual grizzlies. But there is a debate as to whether the black-tailed prairie dog should join the grizzly on the federal list of threatened species. While the political gains of such a listing are debatable, it is clear that our past strategies have failed the prairie dog—and the creatures that depend on it.

Only three states—Wyoming, Montana, and South Dakota—have substantial numbers of black-tailed prairie dogs. No state offers prairie dogs any real legal protection. They can be shot, poisoned, and gassed at will. And, by and large, they are.

Karen and I were on our way to the Manning Corral on the Charles M. Russell Refuge. The plain here is not fry-pan flat, but rather rolls and dips with coulees and draws. We postponed this journey for the evening, when the fence shadow stretched across the prairie. It remained hot. We had been told the deserted ranch outpost supported one of the largest unmolested prairie-dog towns remaining in the West. We drove down a hardscrabble gravel road. The only water in this rangeland is captured in small reservoirs, impounded behind bulldozed berms. Small flocks of pronghorn antelope lingered near these ponds, fidgeting upon our arrival and flushing when we stopped and turned our binoculars on them.

Pronghorn are another creature collected and described by Lewis and Clark. There is no other animal quite like it. The captains could only compare it to the gazelle or antelope of Africa, although the animals are not related. Unlike elk, moose, or bison, pronghorn are creatures solely of North America. "They are a very pretty animal and astonishingly fleet," wrote Lewis in his journal. Clark added in his: "They are all keenly made and are butifull."

Keenly made indeed. Their legs are like spindles turned on evolution's lathe. The bone is honeycombed, offering light weight and remarkable strength. With a flexible spine, and outsize heart and lung capacity, pronghorn can rocket across the plains at sixty miles per hour in bursts and maintain a gallop of forty-five miles per hour. The antelope is far faster than any predator in the modern prairie. The antelope is overbuilt: an Indy 500 race car on a suburban street. They'll smoke any predator out here: coyotes, bears, wolves. On Earth, cheetahs are the only predator approaching their speed.

Indeed, it was the cheetah that resulted in the fleetness of the pronghorn antelope. Prehistoric North America had two species of cheetah, evolutionary prototypes of the African cats. For millions of years, cheetahs coursed pronghorn back and forth across the American plains. Some time in the Pleistocene, the pronghorn won that little race once and for all. Evolution, however, did not prepare the pronghorn for plows, barbed wire, and bullets. By the end of the 1800s, North America's 60 million pronghorn were cut to 13,000. European man almost did what the cheetah and the Ice Age could not: drive the antelope extinct.

But we pulled the antelope back from the brink. Americans imposed hunting restrictions and protected key habitat like the Charles M. Russell Refuge. With money from hunting licenses, antelope were restored to places where they had been exterminated. Today, perhaps a million pronghorn run across the western United States and Canada. What I love about pronghorn, besides their unmatched speed, is their striking markings—white flanks and throat patches on a cinnabar hide, and jetblack facial accents around those deep, globular eyes. The black, barbed daggers of their horns. They are keen-sighted, social animals and are designed to be recognized from a distance. One antelope can spy another miles across the prairie, know instantly what it is and what it is up to. Watching these creatures race across the prairie, I was grateful for every one of them.

Karen and I drove past a ranch house and took a right where our hand-drawn map indicated. With every mile, the road became more rutted and braided—less a road and more a trail. Western road maps are full of old trails: the Lewis and Clark Trail, the Oregon Trail, the Santa Fe Trail, the Outlaw Trail, and the Nez Perce Trail. Their vague lines connect the West that was to the West that is. They may even stretch to the West we imagine will be. But underneath them, there *is* a real West. A place as real as barbed wire, as actual as a pickup truck stuck in a winter ditch.

We want our trails, but we also want places to explore. We desire information and mystery in just the right proportion. We've mapped every last scrap of Earth, but our desire—our instinct— to explore remains unsated. So we explore atoms and the cosmos. Perhaps the allure of exploration lies in the simplicity of a blank map. The places we leave behind are tangled in granny knots of personal and cultural history that we long to escape. But the longer we are at a new place, the more complicated that new venue becomes. However, the delusion was the original sense of simplicity. The new places were complicated from the start. It's just that in the excitement of exploration, we fail to recognize it. When we do see the complexity, we once again long to cut ourselves from it, leave it behind for another, simpler place that must be around here, someplace.

Sagebrush grew thick in the center of the road, brushing the Subaru's undercarriage like steel bristles. The gulch bottoms were caked in barren white, devoid of plants. Alkali flats. That's saline—sea salt—left in local shale by an extinct ocean. It reminds me of the chalky rim around the brim of a cowboy hat. The sign posting the border of the refuge seemed like an existential joke: a sign with no one to read it. We crossed a fence line and continued into the heart of the refuge. Our little Subaru rumbled toward the Missouri River. We stopped where the prairie broke into shale side-canyons, thinly timbered with ponderosa pine and Douglas fir. This was Manning Corral.

Our map showed this bench to be the center of a prairie-dog town. We stopped. The only shade was the shadow on the east side of the Subaru. So we hunched alongside the car and erected the spotting scope. We wore sunglasses and cotton hats with wide brims, but our heads ached anyway. We were told this prairie-dog town contained thousands, perhaps tens of thousands, of black-tailed prairie dogs. "Can't miss them," our source had said. "The place teems with prairie dogs and all the creatures that come along with them."

Trouble was, we could find none. Our binoculars and spotting scope turned up only the open prairie. A pair of kestrel falcons chased a red-tailed hawk out of their territory. Mourning doves collected evening grit from the middle of the road. A distant white dot turned into a buck antelope, watching us from a half-mile away. Grasshoppers clattered about on crispy wings. We walked to the lip of the breaks and stared down at the shimmering water of Fort Peck Reservoir. We checked our map against the few unmistakable landmarks. We were in the right spot.

Not a damn prairie dog on this barren patch of earth.

RANDY MATCHETT carries his shade with him: a big, straw Resistol cowboy hat. White.

Matchett is lean and angular. The hat protects his balding scalp from the carcinogenic sun. A black mustache droops down the corners of his mouth. He was raised in the Great Plains, and sometimes when you're talking to him, when he is thinking of an answer to your question, he glances over your shoulder and looks at the horizon far, far away.

The U.S. Fish and Wildlife Service provides him with a Dodge pickup, also outsize and white. An enormous spotlight perches atop the cab, a million-candlepower cyclops developed for the southern Border Patrol, big enough to direct night traffic at a municipal airport. When you specialize in black-footed ferrets, you work nights.

Matchett maintains an office that he rarely visits at the refuge headquarters in Lewistown, Montana. There, a black-footed ferret is stuffed in a glass cabinet. I saw the specimen and thought immediately of a similar glass case in the Smithsonian Museum of Natural History in Washington, D.C. That cabinet held the faded, crudely stuffed remains of a bird named Martha, the last passenger pigeon. Unlike the passenger pigeon, the black-footed ferret has been given a second, then third, chance against extinction.

Lewis and Clark walked over miles of prairie-dog towns without ever suspecting the existence of the ferret. If Clark had ever caught up with the Crow Indians who stole his horses on the Yellowstone, he might have seen ferret pelts on their dress. But as it turned out, the artist John James Audubon and naturalist John Bachman first recorded the ferret. That was in 1851, making the black-footed ferret one of the last mammals discovered in North America. The ferret is a large, lithe weasel, built for snaking into the burrows of prairie dogs. It is the only ferret of North America. A specialist, the black-footed ferret survives only alongside its chief prey. Some 90 percent of a ferret's diet is prairie dogs. The mice and voles that make up the rest are insufficient to sustain its fiery metabolism.

We met Matchett near Malta, where he was busy building a prerelease center for ferrets—a large cage built on a patch of native prairie. There, young ferrets would be released in the same pen as prairie dogs. The predators would learn to hunt prairie dogs before being released in the wild, hopefully improving their odds of survival.

Matchett led us to a small trailer that had been gutted and converted into a prairie-dog barn. Caged like pudgy hamsters, the prairie dogs awaited a grim but necessary fate. Ferret chow.

When we talked about the relationship between ferrets and prairie dogs, about predation rates and litter sizes, sometimes my tongue would trip. I would say "ferret" when I meant "prairie dog," and vice versa.

"It's OK," Matchett said, "I get them mixed up all the time." The lives of the prairie dog and the ferret—prey and predator— are twisted together like strands of a rope.

"The demise of the ferret directly followed the decline of the prairie dog," Matchett said. "The ferrets disappeared as prairie-dog towns were poisoned or were converted to agriculture."

Prairie dogs eat grass. Cows eat grass. That alone has given ranchers and farmers reason to consider prairie dogs pests. Poisoning efforts—scattering bushels of oats laced with strychnine—began with the formation of the big ranches of the 1880s. By 1915 the poisoning campaigns were subsidized by the federal government and began taking hold.

You can't say we weren't warned. By 1926, observers such as naturalist Ernest Thompson Seton were predicting ecological collapse. By 1960, the number of prairie dogs had been reduced by 98 percent, with the remainder scattered throughout several states. Still the poisoning went on. The remaining prairie-dog towns were insufficient to support ferrets. No one had seen a ferret in years. In 1964, officials at the U.S. Fish and Wildlife Service were preparing to declare the ferret officially extinct. As that debate raged, a ferret colony was discovered in Mellette County, South Dakota. The ferrets weren't quite dead yet.

The ferret colony was small and shrinking. Scientists watched as it foundered. Desperate to stave off extinction, biologists captured the survivors in 1971. The plan was to breed the ferrets in captivity, but within three years the last of those captives died. In 1979 the agency once again discussed closing the books on the ferret.

Then, on September 26, 1981, a night-roaming ranch dog near Meeteetse, Wyoming, brought its owner a strange carcass. The rancher brought the animal to the local taxidermist, who recognized it from a book. The black-footed ferret, like Lazarus, was once again extant.

That Wyoming colony, stricken by disease, also appeared

doomed. This time, however, survivors were collected and successfully hand-reared near Laramie, Wyoming. Later generations were reared in the National Zoo in Washington, D.C., and other captive breeding centers. Today there are roughly one thousand ferrets, most in captivity. Randy Matchett is on the team trying to return those creatures to the wild.

Trouble is, ferrets raised in captivity are often poorly suited for survival in the wild. Of the ferrets released, scores starve or are killed by predators for each one that is lucky enough to survive and have young. Restoring ferrets is like starting a fire on a rainy day—requiring careful tending, feeding, patience, and faith. The goal is to save ferrets. In order to do that, we must conserve the prairie dog.

"When it comes to raising captive ferrets, most of the bugs have been worked out of the system," Matchett said. "Each year, the captive breeding program gets better and better. But where we are behind the eight ball is management of the prairie dog."

Matchett's team has fostered a wild population of a few dozen ferrets on the Charles M. Russell Refuge. Until recently, that colony represented half of the wild black-footed ferrets remaining on Earth. But now, biologists are kindling similar colonies in South Dakota, Arizona, and Wyoming.

The ferrets might just survive, if they can reproduce faster than disease, badgers, bad luck, and coyotes can kill them. Matchett's original plan included jump-starting a second ferret population at Manning Corral. Then one summer morning Matchett discovered, as we did, that those prairie dogs were gone.

"The plague killed them," he told us. "Almost every one."

I thought about that a second: that bacteria carried by a flea could wipe out an entire prairie-dog colony, tens of thousands strong.

"How long did that take?"

"We don't know for sure," he said. "Maybe two weeks. Maybe four."

Plague, on top of everything else, is the last thing the prairie dog—or the ferret—needs.

If Westerners, like the clerk at the Malta supermarket, are ambivalent about ferrets, they are more decided about prairie dogs. Pure and simple, prairie dogs are viewed as varmints—a word derived from *vermin.*

In the modern West, prairie dogs have the same legal standing as exotic weeds. In some states it is illegal to foster prairie dogs on private land, lest they spread to another's pasture. They are officially classified as an agricultural nuisance.

Biology aside, those who want to see the ferret survive have their work cut out for them. For one thing, prairie dogs are seen as handy, challenging targets. Shooting rodents was once seen as harmless diversion for rural boys with .22-caliber rifles. Boys that included myself.

I grew out of it, but not everyone does. Now, heavily armed marksmen come from distant states to shoot prairie dogs. Magazines and websites advertise an entire industry. It's not unusual for a shooter to spend a couple thousand dollars on a rifle good for nothing but shooting prairie dogs.

Karen told Matchett about a T-shirt we had seen in a sporting goods store in Lewistown. On the front was a cartoon prairie dog, painted in a rifle's crosshairs. On the back was a red splatter and the words: "One thousand confirmed kills."

Matchett had seen the shirts. Some of the local kids he hires as summer help wear them to work.

Prairie-dog shooting is banned on the Charles M. Russell Refuge. But on surrounding Bureau of Land Management property—public land, mind you—shooting was until recently actively encouraged. The federal government just lately poisoned prairie dogs off thousands of acres of public grassland elsewhere in the West. The future for prairie dogs on private farmland is even more bleak. Cultivated land is devoid of prairie dogs altogether. Grazing land still hosts some dogs, in spite of everything we throw at them.

Oddly, prairie dogs have become a crop. Ranchers advertise prairie-dog shooting, leasing shooting rights on their land. One rancher told Matchett that with today's low beef prices, prairie dogs were more profitable than cattle. On the impoverished Fort Belknap Indian Reservation, the tribal government charges well-heeled, well-armed white men $110 a year for the right to shoot prairie dogs. Shooters are required to hire guides for $100 a day. Some outsiders object to this arrangement, finding it inconsistent with the writings of Black Elk, Chief Seattle, and Jean Jacques Rousseau. Feel free to criticize—after you've spent ten or twenty winters in an underheated shack on the high plains.

Matchett is a moderate fellow. Whatever recreational shooting says about our attitude toward a native life-form, Matchett refuses to condemn it. On the bright side, he says, shooting fees provide financial incentive for keeping dog towns alive.

"The way I see it, there should be room for both recreational shooting and ferrets," he says.

Recreational shooting (never call it hunting, Matchett says, it's nothing of the sort) takes small change compared to the wholesale slaughter via plow, gas, poison, and even housing sub-divisions. And on top of all that, plague.

Before antibiotics and sanitation, plague killed off much of the human population of Europe. Now, plague poses little threat to humans, but it is still creating ecological havoc. Sylvanic plague is caused by a bacteria and is carried by fleas from rodent to rodent. Biologists suspect shipboard rats introduced plague to North America, perhaps in San Francisco. The disease has worked its way north and east, hitting Montana but not, so far, South Dakota. Prairie dogs and ferrets have no natural immunity against the plague. Nothing in their history has prepared them for it. So they die.

As Manning Corral demonstrated, no refuge boundary can block plague. If one infected flea finds its way to a fledgling ferret colony, it would wipe out the prairie dogs, taking all the ferrets as well. Matchett thinks about this often: Years of work, erased in weeks.

AFTER MATCHETT'S WORKDAY, we met for dinner at a restaurant in Malta, a place with pickup trucks in the lot, wagon wheels along the front door, and oil paintings of cows and horses inside. Matchett took five minutes to cross the dining room, chatting and shaking hands with acquaintances. In these days when federal agents of any type are viewed in the rural United States as suspect outsiders, this struck me as unusual. The good field biologists know that this part of the job—listening and talking with the people who work the land—is more important than any number of articles they may publish in obscure academic journals.

Sliding into the booth, Matchett removed his hat and set it crown-down on the bench beside him. A glance around the restaurant showed that this courtesy is not mandatory. Cowboy country.

The irony, Matchett says, is that cattle and prairie dogs are not mutually exclusive. Prairie dogs evolved under the hooves of millions of bison. Grazing can be a boon to prairie dogs. Likewise, prairie dogs aren't necessarily bad for cattle. Early observers noted big game concentrated in the prairie-dog towns. Prairie dogs mow down the long grass and shrubs, but they give broad-leaved plants a chance to grow. Those forbs are more nutritious and succulent than grass, and that attracts antelope and elk. Studies show cattle grazed on prairie-dog towns put on just as much weight as cattle grazed on pasture without them. But it is a difficult task to persuade people to drop their prejudices. It is difficult to consider that one's father and grandfathers may have been mistaken.

"I don't even try to argue that prairie dogs and cattle can get along," Matchett said. "I put it this way: Can't we agree that we should allow prairie dogs on maybe 1 percent of the landscape? Right now, they have a fraction of 1 percent. Is that too much to ask? One percent?"

So far, it is. And so, the prairie dog dwindles. And the odds remain stacked against the black-footed ferret.

"I'm the eternal optimist. I say we have to keep trying," Matchett says. "Of course, my wife disagrees with me. She doesn't think the ferrets will make it. Sometimes I have my doubts myself. It's going to be a long, tough road."

I wondered what that means for a man who spends three out of four weeks some months tending ferrets on a dark prairie, 150 miles from home.

We talked about the Charles M. Russell Refuge and the inescapable pressure of the cattle industry in both the myth and reality of Montana. Subsidized grazing is a long-standing tradition, even on a refuge designated as protected habitat for pronghorn antelope and sharptail grouse.

"We are essentially a well-managed cattle ranch," he said. "The refuge supports three times the biomass of cattle than all the native ungulates combined."

Translation: The wildlife refuge grows three pounds of beef for every pound of elk, bighorn sheep, pronghorn, whitetail, and mule deer, combined. And that's on a *wildlife* refuge. The grazing pressure on other public lands is even higher. Fees for leases are laughably low. Public servants who try to reform these policies run afoul of Western politicians and truncate their careers.

"It's changing," Matchett said, "but change is slow." The waitress arrived and took our orders. Matchett ordered a hamburger. I ordered the chicken-fried steak. Karen ordered a trip through the salad bar.

After dinner, we stepped outside. The western sky was smeared a vivid red, a gauze of clouds promising a break to the heat. Or perhaps just teasing. The land spread beyond the restaurant and beyond the town, beyond the fields to the rough country on the cultivated fringe and to the distant island mountain ranges. An Amtrak train—the Empire Builder—sped down the Hi Line with a load of tourists heading for Glacier National Park and Seattle. Running late. The low evening sun reflected boldly in the oversize windows of the passenger cars.

I thought of the passenger trains of the 1870s. To break the monotony of travel, passengers pointed rifles and pistols out the windows and fired into herds of bison that happened near the track. The carcasses were left to feed coyotes. The shooting did not doom the bison to extinction, but such casual waste contributed to their sharp decline. Bison were the varmints of their day. Today we settle for prairie dogs. The only difference is the size of the target.

From Malta at sunset, the landscape looms large. The fields and grasslands roll to the horizon. Somehow over my lifetime I had come to accept that the great bison herds were a rational trade-off—the cost of converting the plains into a grain garden that feeds the world. Civilization demands farms. Farms demand space. Bison made way. But if our civilization isn't big enough for the ferret and the prairie dog, we must be a small people indeed.

Chapter 3

Grizzlies for the Twenty-First Century

GRIZZLY BEAR
Ursus arctos

EVERY GRIZZLY BEAR, JOHN WALLER SAID, REACTS differently to being caught in a trap. This one didn't like it a bit.

Trying to find grizzly bears along the Lewis and Clark Trail posed a problem. Namely, the bears can no longer be found anywhere along the explorers' four-thousand-mile route. So that led us to the Quintonken Creek drainage of the Flathead National Forest, a few miles outside Montana's Bob Marshall Wilderness. It was early morning on an empty forest road.

Waller reached into the cab of his pickup and extracted a stubby-barreled shotgun. He loaded a handful of cartridges, and a quick pump of the action slammed one round into the chamber. Waller had the kind of youthful face that earned the suspicion of bartenders years after he passed the legal drinking age. He wore the uniform of this trapping team: khaki button-down shirt with a blue ball cap. The shoulder of the shirt and the forehead of the cap show an embroidered grizzly bear, the logo of the Montana Department of Fish, Wildlife and Parks. The wildlife agency of California boasts a similar patch. But Montana, unlike California, has grizzlies in its woods and not just on the logo. Waller was raised in suburban Maryland, but wears cowboy-style Wrangler jeans and a saucer-size belt buckle that could have been a runner-up award at a rodeo. As a kid, he watched Marlin Perkins catch bears on Sunday nights on Mutual of Omaha's *Wild Kingdom.*

We visited Waller in June. The rich smell of spring forest was only occasionally overwhelmed by a rank whiff of roadkill—the bait that lured the grizzly into this predicament.

We were here to catch grizzlies. Waller was a graduate student and a trapper working on a ten-year research project. The bawling bear was the latest subject of that research. The idea was to shoot the bear with a tranquilizer dart while at all costs not shooting it with Waller's chrome shotgun. We could not, at the moment, see this bear. We could only hear the rhythmic, throaty moans of ursine despair. She was tethered to a tree by a steel cable. The bear experts say the threat posed by an unprovoked grizzly bear is universally overrated. The unprovoked bear would rather flee than fight, virtually every time. Trouble is, trapping a grizzly is a provocation if anything ever was. One of the earliest fatal maulings in Yellowstone National Park was of a poacher who trapped a grizzly in the northern edge of the park. As the poacher closed in to finish off the captured animal, the bear charged and broke the trap chain. The bear, slowed by the heavy steel trap, killed the poacher and then bit the man's rifle in two.

Our bear was hidden in this messy, even chaotic, forest. The cover was dense subalpine fir and Engelmann spruce—both live and standing, and dead and fallen. Mountain ash and Sitka alder wove an impenetrable curtain of stem and leaf, reinforced by a nasty plant called devil's club. Alder and ash slap your face and gouge your eyes, but the thorns of devil's club perforate the palms of your hands. These mountains are a cold jungle; a rain forest that receives half its precipitation in snow. This was a wild land, but not true wilderness. It was public forest traditionally dedicated to the growth of trees for timber. Narrow dirt roads carved by bulldozers wiggled up every canyon, leading to great, square clear-cuts in various stages of second growth.

Grizzlies and wolverines live reticent lives here. Airplanes crash in this mountain range and sometimes are never found, swallowed up in the thick net of plants. Karen and I drove fifty miles on dirt roads to the government shack along Quintonken Creek. But the topography is deceiving. The nearest home was only fifteen miles away, as the crow flies. Or as the bear walks. This is the netherworld we have left for modern grizzly bears: a wedge between the wild and the domestic.

We met the trappers at their bunkhouse, to tag along the next morning. Karen took a lower bunk while I climbed into the upper.

The bunks were outfitted with old-fashioned mattresses, the kind with buttons sewn on the face. As I spread out my sleeping bag, I noticed each depression in the mattress was full of mouse shit, stained hantaviral yellow. Cripes, I thought. These people are so busy catching bears they can't trap a few mice?

CATCHING GRIZZLY BEARS is not altogether different than trapping mice, aside from the obvious complications of capturing the former alive and kicking. You arrange the bait. You set the trap. You wait. Each morning, the six trappers split into three teams. Each team has a trapline of a dozen or so sets. Karen went with one team; I climbed in the truck with Waller and another grad student, Tom Baumeister. Our time was limited and odds were against any of us catching a bear, so Karen and I spread our bets across the board.

We drove between traps in a GMC pickup, with a little electronic box on the seat between us. The box beeped with the signals from radio-collared bears. Aside from the bears in the traps, or a bear that might dash across the road in front of the trappers, the beeps are often the only sign Waller ever has of these grizzlies. The citizens band radio was also on. The chatter from the local city police department broke the silence between traps, and we eavesdropped on the cop-talk. I knew some police code: 10-21 means a drunk driver, 10-51 is a domestic dispute in progress. For Waller and Baumeister, this information added significant detail to the miniature dramas of the airwaves, dramas unfolding just over the mountains but seemingly in another world.

Instead of cheese, our bait was roadkill. Hooves and legs of dismembered elk and deer jutted from the truck bed. Be thankful the smell cannot be described on paper. Bears smelled us drive by, a mile away. Each piece of bait was hung from a tree, in theory just beyond a bear's reach. The traps were steel cable, anchored to a tree. The noose was the size of a dinner plate, buried carefully in the forest duff. Each bait hosted a pair of hidden snares. When Waller set or checked his snares, he pulled on rubber gloves and boots to keep his scent off the ground. The snare was connected to a steel stake, driven into the ground like a tent peg. This stake was a spring trigger. When a paw stepped on the trigger, the snare coiled tight around the animal's wrist or ankle. When the snare was ready, Waller sprinkled duff and moss over the loop and patted it gently until it became invisible.

Every spring for a decade, the crew had run these traplines, under the guidance of research biologist Rick Mace. In all, they had captured more than fifty grizzly bears, most more than once. The object was to trap as many grizzlies as possible in the Swan Mountain study area, fixing the animals with radio collars and ear tags. Then the team regularly checked on those bears, by over-flights and with automatic cameras hidden strategically throughout the woods. The objective, roughly put, was to see how well humans and bears are sharing this piece of woods. I was not completely at ease with modern grizzly research. It saddened me that our last grizzlies are trapped, drugged, jabbed, prodded, and pierced, their privates invaded with a thermometer. That they awaken adorned with fluorescent plastic, their blood drawn for DNA fingerprinting, and their lips tattooed for future identification. They are identified by number and dogged by government aircraft—and now even satellite. Their motions are recorded in a distant computer. It's Marlin Perkins meets George Orwell.

"Is all this really necessary?" Karen asked me during a private moment. "Why not just let the bears be?" The bluntest answer came from Maurice Hornocker, a pioneer of radiotelemetry and a world authority on big cats. "The alternative," Hornocker told me, "is ignorance."

And ignorance has never served the grizzly bear well.

IT IS EASY to forget that many animals we consider Western—bison, elk, cougar, wolf—were once creatures of the Eastern seaboard. Because the East is more lush than the West, precolonial Virginia probably contained more elk and bison per acre than, say, Wyoming does now. But grizzly bears were true animals of the West.

Other European explorers saw grizzlies long before Lewis and Clark explored the Louisiana Purchase. Henry Kelsey saw grizzlies in Manitoba in 1602. Father Antonio de la Acension, a Spaniard, wrote of grizzlies in the American Southwest in 1691. But the great bear was introduced to the collective imagination of the United States by the heady adventures of Lewis and Clark. The Corps found grizzly tracks in the banks of the Missouri River in South Dakota in the fall of 1804. Immediately, they knew the beast that left these tracks was different from the shy black bear they knew back in the East. The tracks were pigeon-toed and flat-footed, with claws that scratched three inches beyond each toe. The tracks resembled a giant moccasin print, laden with a lethal kinesis.

While waiting out the winter of 1804-05 with the Mandans, the Corps of Discovery heard the Indians' bear stories. Lewis noted that the Mandans treated the grizzly with "supersticious rites." A Mandan going on a bear hunt acted similarly to a warrior going off to battle, Lewis wrote. The Indians spoke with awe of the power of these bears. Initially, Lewis downplayed the potential danger. He figured Indians, little more than stone-age archers, were simply outmatched. "The Indians may well fear this anamal, equiped as they generally are with their bows and arrows . . . but in the hands of a skillfull rifleman they are by no means as formidable or dangerous as they have been represented."

But really, what did he know?

In April 1805, in North Dakota, the Corps's hunters finally saw grizzly bears. They flushed them out of a riverside copse when they opened fire on a herd of elk. These first grizzlies ran like rabbits, loping for the nearest horizon. But these grizzlies were not the bears the hero-explorers bragged about upon their return to Washington in 1806. Nor are they the grizzlies we associate with the Voyage of Discovery today.

The Corps killed its first grizzly—that is "collected" its first grizzly specimen—along Big Muddy Creek in the far northeast corner of Montana. On the morning of April 29, 1805, Lewis and another hunter caught a pair of grizzlies unaware. They singled out a three-hundred-pound bear and stalked it. The first shots only wounded the bear, probably breaking a shoulder. In a fury of pain and confusion, the wounded bear charged the hunters, chasing them seventy yards. A healthy grizzly will easily outrun any man, but this one was wounded sufficiently to give Lewis and his partner time to ram new loads down their awkward, muzzle-loading rifles. They shot again and finished the bear. The explorers soon learned they were in for more than they bargained for.

In early May, Clark and George Drouillard stalked another bear. It was, Clark wrote, "a verry large and a turrible looking animal, which we found verry hard to kill." They shot the bear ten times—five rifle balls blowing half-inch holes in the animal's lungs. The wounded bear gave a roar, took to the river, and swam to a sandbar. It took twenty minutes for the animal to bleed to death. Many of the grizzlies the Corps shot tried to return the favor and kill the explorers. Over and over again, wounded bears charged. Explorers fled. They leaped off the cutbanks of the Missouri, waded into the water or scrambled up trees. They did not know the first rule when encountering grizzlies, a rule that experience dictates but instinct screams against: Do not run. Never run.

Over and over, the captains marveled how these bears withstood brutal punishment. "The wonderful power of life which these animals possess renders them dreadful," Clark wrote. The men took to stalking the bears in squadrons. Half the group would shoot at once, firing a volley of four or five shots, while the rest held their fire. When the wounded bear charged, the second group would open fire while the others raced to reload. Soon, Lewis revised his views of this animal: "These bear being so hard to die reather intimedates us all . . . I must confess I do not like the gentleman and had reather fight two Indians than one bear."

Lewis described another grizzly with more artistic flair than scientific objectivity as "a monster animal, a terrible enemy." The bears particularly terrified the explorers at White Bear Islands, near the Great Falls of the Missouri. The bears entered their camps at night, although they did not hurt anyone. The river was littered with bison carcasses, which attracted scavenging grizzlies. The scene was probably similar to today's McNeil River, Alaska, where up to thirty brown bears will gather at a time to fish for salmon. Lewis figured the great bears were used to defending their "right of soil" in the neighborhood.

The expedition's best bear story took place at White Bear Islands and involved Pvt. Hugh McNeal, during the homeward journey of 1806. The Corps had split up, with Clark heading for the Yellowstone River while Lewis was back at the Great Falls. McNeal was with Lewis, camped at White Bear Islands. McNeal was riding alone through thick brush when his horse surprised a grizzly bear only ten feet away. The horse bucked and turned, throwing McNeal to the ground at the bear's feet. The bear must have been as surprised as McNeal, for the man had time to stand, grab his musket, and swing it like a club. He cracked the weapon over the bear's broad skull, splitting the animal's scalp and breaking the gun. As the bear clutched at its wounded head, McNeal scrambled up a tree. The bear kept McNeal treed until nearly sundown. Eventually the bear wandered off, allowing McNeal to drop down, collect his battered weapon, and search for his horse.

The explorers described their bear specimens in detail. They measured each bear's dimensions to the half-inch and refrained from exaggeration when guessing an animal's weight. They found the grizzly both larger and more aggressive than any predator they had ever encountered, and indeed, it is the largest carnivore in North America and among the largest in the world. "The heart being equal to that of a large ox," Lewis wrote. "His maw is ten times larger."

Lewis and Clark were a bit baffled by the fact that grizzlies come in a variety of colors, as do western varieties of the so-called black bears. At first they called grizzlies *white bears*. Silvertip grizzlies can almost glow white, particularly when viewed from a distance and backlit by the sun. But grizzlies can just as easily be coal black or any shade in between. Only one mammal on Earth varies in color more than the grizzly, *Ursus arctos.* That is the black bear, *Ursus americanus.*

"I am induced to believe that the Brown, the white and the Grizzly bear of this country are the same species, only differing in color," Lewis wrote. "They may be called white black grizzly brown or red bear, for they are found in all those colors. Perhaps it would not be unappropriate to call them the variagated bear."

Clark cut through the confusion by calling a specimen "a bear of the large vicious species."

Any newcomer to grizzly country, from Meriwether Lewis at Big Muddy Creek to a Yellowstone tourist on Mount Washburn, has much to learn. Grizzly country demands certain manners. In part, the Corps found trouble because its members were unaware of this protocol. They did not know how to avoid bedding areas during the day or feeding areas at dawn and dusk, or that fleeing from a bear only triggers the chase. Eventually they learned to avoid grizzlies altogether, rather than pick fights with them. They learned the hard way. Perhaps the Mandans knew these things—but the explorers had dismissed their "supersticious rites." Instead, the Corps put its faith in firepower. The expedition killed forty-three grizzlies. That set the precedent for the next two hundred years.

Most often, Waller's traps are empty. Waller will load his riot gun and walk away from the protection of the pickup truck and into the tangled forest. The deer haunch will dangle from the tree unmolested. The snares will be where he buried them. On average he will do this eighty times in a row. Then, the eighty-first time, the snare will hold a bear.

From that moment, all predictions are off. Grizzlies are used to great freedom and, as a rule, do not take kindly to having their liberties curtailed. Bears are individualists, Waller said. It is unwise to assume they will act in any predictable manner.

Some bears you do not catch at all. Or maybe you catch a bear once, and that's all the education that bear needs. One such animal was No. 146. The young bear was first captured in a traditional culvert trap—a bulky, box-trap affair made of a steel pipe welded to a trailer frame and towed behind a pickup. When the team wanted to replace his collar, they set another culvert trap. The bear visited at night. He tipped the trap over as if with disdain. The trappers gave up with culvert traps and tried the spring-loaded snares, which are more difficult to detect. Waller boiled the snares to kill any residual scent. He wore rubber gloves and boots. He set the snares carefully. He patted the duff carefully. The works.

Bear 146 did not ignore these traps. He scorned them. He did not avoid them: He sprung them. He sprung them as if he obtained joy from the very act. And then he took the bait. This went on, over and over, for years. Traps set. Snares sprung. Bait stolen. Bear free. The trappers figured the bear was picking up rocks or logs in his mouth and dropping them on the snares. Vexed, Waller tried saturation trapping. The team set twenty-two snares around a hanging bait, using all the cable they could spare. Waller believed the bear could not possibly keep track of all those hidden traps. At the least, the bear would place a rear paw in one snare while disabling another. Waller was wrong. Bear 146 tripped every single snare. All twenty-two.

Bear 146 may still be out there. Waller would like to catch him
to learn a little piece of what No. 146 knows. On the other hand,
he likes to think there is a bear that cannot be caught. But No. 146
is exceptional. Most are mortal. Some are suckers for the bait and
get caught over and over again. They're caught so often they get in
the way. Some are cagey, but make mistakes. Run out of luck.

Once ensnared, a grizzly may vent its rage by dismembering
whatever tree is in reach. Trap sites are standing exhibits of animal
fury: Tree bark is torn clean from the trunks; the trunks suffer
jagged bites that sink straight to the heartwood. Others dig, as if
to escape by burrowing deep trenches through rocks and roots.
When you approach these bears, you see nothing but fuzzy round
ears above the torn earth. Still other bears seem to wait with gentle patience, as if knowing the trappers will arrive soon to set
them free. Some trapped bears fall sound asleep out of boredom.
Other bears wait quietly, as if in ambush. They charge at the last
moment with terrible racehorse speed. In these cases the trapper
must hold his ground, stay beyond the reach of the cable, hoping
the steel doesn't snap or the anchor tree does not uproot. Trapping
grizzly bears is not a task to be taken lightly.

AS OUR BEAR BAWLED FROM THE THICKET, John Waller stepped
from the pickup truck and joined his partners, Erik Wenum, Eric
Schmidt, and Terry Werner. We had regrouped, each member con-
tacted by radio.

Wenum set a tackle box on the pickup tailgate and flipped
open the lid. The trays were laden with tranquilizing drugs and

hypodermic needles in sterile dressings. Wenum snapped on latex gloves and loaded a syringe, tapping an air bubble out of the shaft with his fingernail. The dart had a yarn tassel like a yellow marigold. Wenum loaded the dart into an air rifle. The drug was Telazol, a muscle relaxant that renders the animal immobile but does not technically knock it unconscious. The drugged animal senses what is going on, but is powerless to react. Waller waited with his shotgun. This team has caught, radio-collared, and released grizzly bears more than one hundred times without ever having to kill one in the process. In fact, during all those captures, only three bears have suffered so much as minor cuts from the snare. No trappers have been harmed. The process does entail some risk, mostly for the bears. Early in the project, a poacher beat the trappers to a site and killed an ensnared grizzly. Another young grizzly was killed by a dominant male bear shortly after it was released from the trap, probably while the smaller animal was still groggy from the tranquilizer.

Not to say there aren't tense moments for the trappers as well. Just the previous week, a trap held an adult female while her mate was still free in the woods. The male charged the trappers when they approached. A trapper fired one warning round over the big male's head and would have aimed lower and fired again if the bear had continued his charge. When I asked about these moments, I came to understand that the death of a bear was the ultimate failure, almost akin to a surgeon watching a patient die under anesthesia. "If there were any other way to do this besides trapping bears," John said, "we would do it."

◆

GRIZZLIES EVOLVED in the Pleistocene, one more predator in a tough neighborhood. A bear struggling to survive had a couple options: become shy and learn to climb trees like the black bear, or stand its ground. Every animal has a switch in its brain to direct its body to fight or flee. The grizzly's switch is tuned a little closer to *fight* than what we are used to.

There is one other thing we think about, when we think about grizzlies. The grizzly will, upon rare occasion, view human beings as mere prey. In the modern world, we are killed by viruses and bacteria. It is unusual to fall prey to an organism larger than ourselves. It upsets our preconceptions about the order of the world and our place in it.

It chills the base of the brain to read rangers' reports about the fatal bear maulings that occasionally occur in our national parks. Take one night in August 1967 in Glacier National Park. A small group of young hikers slept around a campfire near Trout Lake, a day's hike from the nearest road. A bear invaded their camp, looking for food. The campers scrambled for cover, but Michele Koons was trapped in her sleeping bag by a jammed zipper. Her companions listened from nearby trees, like baboons trapped by a night-stalking leopard. The bear dismembered the young woman before her own eyes. "It's got my arm off," were her last words. "Oh God. I'm dead."

In 1993, another hiker was killed and eaten by a sow grizzly and two cubs in Glacier Park. Rick Mace and this trapping team were called in to snare the bears. Mace caught grizzlies all right, but never the right ones. Eventually the bear family was gunned down by rangers in a helicopter. Mace says running that trapline was one of the spookiest chores in his career.

Even in Glacier Park, with its reputation for man-eating grizzlies, many more visitors drown in frigid lakes or are swept over waterfalls than are killed by bears. Cars cause far more trauma than claws. The rare cases of predation almost always involve bears that have an unnatural diet of campground garbage. Like all healthy organisms, bears love life too much to squander it on conflict. A grizzly will avoid a thousand conflicts—maybe ten thousand—for every time it stands and fights. Unfortunately the bear never gets credit for conflicts avoided. He makes headlines every time he wades into a fight. And the grizzly will fight with less reluctance than most North American mammals. While this trait should never be exaggerated, it is no doubt what lends the bear its unmatched authority and power in our imagination.

The grizzlies encountered by the Corps of Discovery were substantially different creatures than those studied by Rick Mace's team. The Great Plains grizzly followed bison migrations through present-day Kansas and Nebraska. The bears finished off the cripples, the aged, and the weak, chased wolves from their kills and feasted on the newborn calves. Bison drowned by the score crossing the Missouri, the Yellowstone, and the Platte, and their wealth of carcasses must have attracted grizzlies from many miles away.

There is an active, if moot, biological debate as to whether grizzlies were poised to expand east of the Mississippi River in 1800. We know they roamed the entire North American cordillera, south into Mexico and to the beaches near Monterey and San Francisco. But when civilizing forces arrived, grizzlies were the first to go. They were eliminated first from the cultivated lowlands, then from the mountains. From the Sierra Nevada, the San Juans, the Wasatch Range, the Cascades, the Sawtooths, the

Sierra Madre, the Wallowas. Bold bears were, in Darwinian parlance, selected against. The survivors learned to run and hide. By the mid-1880s, outdoor writers like Teddy Roosevelt and George Bird Grinnell bemoaned the fact that grizzlies were not as ferocious as they were one hundred years before. The animals, they said, were somehow reduced. The animal's mettle (and the ability to measure one's manhood against it) was another fragment of wilderness fed to the voracious engine of Manifest Destiny.

There were probably about fifty thousand grizzlies south of the forty-ninth parallel in 1805. Today, there are perhaps one thousand. But those numbers are suspect. Grizzly bears, as this team of researchers demonstrates, are difficult beasts to count. Grizzlies remain where there is enough wild country to support them. Quintonken Creek is in what bear biologists call the Northern Continental Divide Ecosystem, surrounding the Bob Marshall Wilderness and Glacier National Park. It is one of two places south of Canada where somewhat healthy grizzly bear populations remain. The second population is around Yellowstone National Park. Today, the bears that Mace studies are even more shy, more retiring than any previous generation. This is particularly true of sows with cubs. They eke out a living in the wildest corners of these mountains, rarely even seen for all the rock and brush. They are smaller, too, from their vegetarian rations. More than 90 percent of their diet is huckleberries, cow parsnip, and other plants.

Some bear experts—Rick Mace and John Waller among them—believe that bears become more shy and retiring when they are conditioned to rifle fire. Some observers believe grizzly bears inside the sanctuary of national parks carry more of their natural boldness than animals like those Mace studies, which have withstood generations of hunting and persecution. However, our collective mythology about the ferocity of grizzly bears has probably always been inflated. Roosevelt and Grinnell remembered the wounded bears that charged Lewis and Clark, but dismissed the grizzlies that fled from them. Because of our myths about grizzlies, we eradicated the bears with the same vigor with which we later eradicated the smallpox virus. In our wake, we have left the West a poorer place.

THE TRAPPERS CREPT IN FOR A LOOK. They recognized the bawling bear—a two-year-old female. They followed her mother three years ago, when she was courted and mated by the Swan Range males. They watched the sow emerge from its winter den with two tiny cubs in tow. They knew that this summer, these two twins would be on their own for the first time. A year ago, her moans might have elicited a quick defense from her mother. This summer, however, the mother was ready to mate once again. She was off looking for a male. At least, we hoped she was. "You guys," Waller said to me and Karen, "will stay at the truck."

Officials of the Montana Department of Fish, Wildlife and Parks are edgy about taking laymen along on bear-trapping forays. A few years before disaster struck on a similar outing. A warden was assigned to release a bear that had been raiding rural orchards. It was a big male, quite agitated inside the culvert traps. As it so happened, a group of outdoors journalists were in town, and the warden invited several to come along. All began as planned. The warden drove the culvert trap to a predetermined spot in the backcountry. The photographers lined up and focused their cameras on the trap. But the trapdoor jammed. So the warden crawled on top of the trap to free the door.

The bear tumbled out of the trap and wheeled on release. The six-hundred-pound bear swiped the two-hundred-pound warden out of the back of the pickup. The bear bit and clawed the warden as the terrified man emptied his .44 revolver, point blank, into the animal. The sixth bullet broke the bear's spine. After a brief hospital stay, the warden lived. The bear died. All in a clatter of camera shutters. Since then, anyone not on the trapping team is required to stay in the nearest car until the bear is drugged. We didn't argue.

The trappers stepped behind the forest curtain. Our ears strained for clues of what was going on. In the thicket, the moaning stopped. Then came a *pop*, like a bottle uncorked, followed by an unmistakable yowl. A few minutes later, the trappers emerged from the underbrush, carrying the limp bear in a canvas tarpaulin.

They lay the bear gently on the ground behind the pickup. The animal looked deflated, like a rug. She was a lovely, golden-flanked animal with chocolate legs and a line of brown fur running over the distinctive grizzly hump of her shoulders. In magazines and on television, bears are always majestic and enormous. And they can be. In reality, though, bears vary. This one looked as ferocious as a golden retriever. Someday she might reach four hundred pounds at maturity on a diet of huckleberries and cow parsnip. Bears grow larger yet, particularly if they luck into a protein diet. A stock-fed bruiser on the Blackfeet Indian Reservation, just east of here, recently topped eight hundred pounds. Grizzly cubs are born in the winter dens, weighing only about one pound at birth. If humans had a similar birth-to-maturity size ratio, a typical infant would weigh three tons by the time he was thirty-five.

This drugged bear exhaled a heavy sigh, like the *huff* of a drunk passed out in an easy chair. I was sorely tempted to touch her fur, thick even this late into spring, and feel her rib cage rise and fall. (To pet a living grizzly!) I refrained, recalling she was conscious and perhaps terrified. We whispered, as if we might startle her awake. The first thing to go on was the radio collar. That way, if the drug suddenly wore off and we all had to dash for the truck, the capture would not be a complete loss. Waller dabbed the bear's eyes with ointment, then tied a bandanna over her face. Eric Schmidt opened a metal clipboard while Erik Wenum stretched a measuring tape around the prone animal, measuring the girth of her chest. From this measurement, her weight could be accurately estimated. The tape revealed the length of the head and width of a paw. (These are much the same measurements Lewis took on his trophies.) Schmidt drew a blood sample, checked the animal's temperature.

What struck me were the fore-claws, long and curved like those of a giant badger. While bears are often credited for their strength and intelligence, they are also remarkably dexterous. At a Forest Service trailhead near here, another young sow grizzly made an industry of breaking into parked pickup trucks, stealing sack lunches and oat pellets from inside. Toward the inevitable end of her career, she was so skilled that she could break into a truck *without breaking glass.* She hooked those wonderful claws in the windshield and pulled out the weather stripping as if it were a long piece of black licorice. She then popped the windshield free, laid it over the hood, and raided the cab. I am convinced that if grizzlies had evolved opposable thumbs, they would be the ones studying us and we would be the ones hiding in the mountains.

The team worked seriously and quickly. When the data sheets were filled and the bear was outfitted with its hardware, two men remained behind to make certain the bear awoke safely, while the others left to check the remaining traplines. On average, the trapping team caught one bear every three days. This was no average day. By nightfall the team added three more grizzlies to their sample. We did not regroup at the shack at Quintonken Creek until well after dark.

I MET RICK MACE at his cubicle at the state wildlife agency headquarters in Kalispell, Montana. The stuffed head of a grizzly snarled from one wall, its marble eyes staring at Mace's high-octane computer. Mace frequently wears a plastic armband on his wrist. Repetitive-motion syndrome is chronic with bear trappers and other computer jocks. Outside his window, beyond the parking lot and power lines, one can see the peaks of the northern Swan Range. These mountains are his study area, where the bears roam. Inside his computer, the bears' peregrinations are stored in silicon chips. Montana is full of self-proclaimed grizzly experts who base their conclusions on anecdotes or observations or legends or books or folklore. But Mace believes in data. And that he has by the gigabyte.

In the ten years of this project, Mace will follow more than fifty bears, watching them mate, give birth, and die. He and Waller will fly over the Swan Range in a Cessna twice a week, as allowed by the moods of Montana weather. Wenum will follow discreetly on the ground, downloading data on a laptop, carrying camping gear and extra batteries aboard a pack llama. They will collect some forty-four hundred signals from the radio collars. The research will show, among other things, that this particular population of bears is on a slight decline, the death rate somewhat greater than the birth rate.

Indeed, the twin sister of the little bear we trapped was found dead a few weeks after our visit. Like most of the bears that died during Mace's study, she died of a peculiar disease introduced to American grizzlies by Lewis and Clark on April 29, 1805. It's a disease that pushed the bear onto the federal list of threatened species in 1974: physical trauma caused by gunshot.

Mace explained to me some of the things his research had shown. For years, the Forest Service in this corner of Montana used the grizzly bear as part of its rationale for cutting timber. The bureaucratic logic went like this: Clear-cuts grow back in huckleberries, and grizzly bears like huckleberries, thus clear-cuts help grizzly bears. This alleged symbiosis between chain saw and bear suited the timber industry and the Forest Service alike, prompting ample sales of subsidized federal timber. The trouble was, no one asked the bears about it. Until Mace came along.

Mace found that bears occasionally fed in clear-cuts. But not as much as one might expect. While clear-cuts may produce huckleberries, the accompanying roads and traffic prompt the grizzlies to avoid those areas. The rifle-toting humans on those roads make the places dangerous for bears. Logging itself—that is, cutting trees—was probably neutral for the bears. The problem came from the roads and humans on them, Mace found.

However, the backcountry like Quintonken Creek was only part of the picture. These bears live split lives: part in the wilds and part out. For years Rick Mace has followed a 650-pound male grizzly, one of the largest ever recorded in Montana and the largest he has ever trapped. Bear No. 22, known as Digger, lives part of his life in the Bob Marshall Wilderness. In autumn, apple orchards prove irresistible. The owner of one orchard—an older, exceptionally tolerant fellow—doesn't mind the bear. He enjoys catching glimpses of Digger on October evenings. But now the artsy tourist town of Bigfork has closed in on the orchard. Digger dozes away his autumn afternoons in the woodlot behind the Dairy Queen. When he walks across the road, his claws tap on asphalt. Digger is a sly, nocturnal bear who knows his business well. But he scares people. So his life is fraught with danger; someday, someone may very well shoot him. And that, in the end, is the problem. The threats differ in different habitats, but they boil down to people and bears vying for the same territory. No matter if it's 1805 or 2005.

On the Rocky Mountain Front and the Blackfeet Indian Reservation, the issue is ranching: Bears prey on calves, lambs, even honeybees. Around Yellowstone Park, bears run afoul of elk hunters or backpackers, breaking into camps for their food, and end up dead or shipped to zoos. Along the south end of Glacier Park, bears are attracted by grain spilled along the railroad tracks and are killed by freight trains. Elsewhere, a flood of latter-day homesteaders, telecommuters, and retirees seek solitude on five-acre, backwoods ranchettes. Bears eat trash left on the back porch, dog food out of Rover's dish, or birdseed left out for chickadees. Then the homeowners demand that the state game warden trap the bear and haul it to the backcountry so they can enjoy their woods without worry. But every year, there is less and less backcountry.

There are some treaties in this proxy war: We do not shoot

grizzlies as quickly as we once did; we do not poison them; although pressure is continuous, we refrain from some grazing, mining, and logging in the remaining fragments of grizzly bear habitat. At least on public land, industry is given something less than free rein. But other threats—particularly the use of bear habitat for summer cabins and second homes—are hardly being addressed. Most of the bear deaths that Mace recorded occurred when they ventured into the lowlands, raiding trash cans like overgrown raccoons. There is evidence that the number of bears is growing, particularly in protected sanctuaries like Yellowstone and Glacier National Parks. But grizzly country is becoming more crowded with humans, pressed more tightly by industry, more fragmented by impassable highways. There is no place in the lower forty-eight states that is more than twenty miles from a road—and a grizzly will walk twenty miles on an afternoon whim.

We may be confident about the grizzly's future in the short run, but the distant horizon remains foggy. Enough of us value the power and the presence of the grizzly to pass laws in its behalf. Laws that, if courageously enforced and publicly supported, might give the grizzly a chance.

"Consider this," Rick Mace said. "Eighty years ago, there were grizzlies leaving their tracks on the beaches, right outside Los Angeles. Eighty years ago. I bet you have a living grandparent who was alive eighty years ago. Los Angeles is a different place now. Our job is to look ahead, eighty years from now."

ON THE FOURTH OF JULY, Karen and I hiked into the Swan Mountains, just north of Quintonken Creek. The trail started in a dense canopy of spruce, but climbed gradually to timberline. In spite of the date, we found snow on the ground. Gobs of it. Early in the day, the snow was solid enough to support our weight. We walked on it as we would a sidewalk. But as the afternoon warmed, the snow melted to mush. We sank to our knees, stepped up, then punched through again. The crust cut our naked calves, and snow trickled down the tops of our boots. Walking became exhausting.

The path led to a cirque dotted with alpine lakes, most still iced over. We found Birch Lake half-enclosed with ice. In the patch of open water, little planter trout rose to a minuscule hatch of aquatic insects. We could walk no farther without snowshoes. We found a patch of earth large and flat enough to claim for a tent. Our camp was perched above the lake, the windblown slope of Mount Aeneas behind us.

Karen pointed out three mountain goats on an outcrop near the summit—old whitebeards, with black daggers atop their heads. They appeared prehistoric, gazing down on this icy land, their fur matted and dingy in midsummer molt. Lewis and Clark saw them like this, in the distance.

Toward dusk I fidgeted with my moody backpacking stove, trying to coax a pot of water to boil for pasta. The fuel line was clogged, and the blue flame sputtered out as soon as I could light it. I was hungry, and not fond of crunchy noodles. Karen was in the tent, putting on long pants for the evening. I looked up from the stove, finding Mount Aeneas cut in sharp detail by the evening light. I scanned for the goats but instead found a bronze spot moving slowly across the mountainside.

"Karen," I called, "where's the spotting scope?" She knew by my voice that I was watching a grizzly. The scope revealed a full-bodied animal with dark legs and a blond ridge on her humped shoulder. An adult bear ambling across the mountain, clearly not the overgrown cub we snared with the trap team. Her profile was that of a grand piano with the top propped open. Her fur ruffled luxuriantly in the mountain breeze. She dipped into timber, then emerged again to nibble glacier lilies or bust a log for ant larvae.

It is difficult to objectively describe a grizzly because it is so many things. The grizzly is the nightmare man-eater the tourists fear at Yellowstone and the Teddy bear you slept with as a child; it is the largest carnivore on land and an overgrown ground squirrel nibbling on wildflower roots; it is the icon of the former Soviet threat, symbol of hard times on Wall Street, mascot from the California state flag or Chicago football pennant; it is the proto-Christ, arising from its cave-tomb after winter's death. It is *Ursus arctos* of scientific journals; it is Real Bear of Blackfeet legend; it is the "monster animal" and "terrible enemy" in Lewis's journal; and it is an amalgamation of zeros and ones in a biologist's computer file. It is the walking embodiment of wilderness. But it is never simply a bear.

As we watched, this bear meandered toward the mountain goats. With every step the bear took toward the outcrop, we expected the goats to flee in terror. But instead, it was the bear that turned and ran in its back-heavy bear gait. The bear went over the mountain. The goats remained behind and resumed their evening feed. When we cranked the telescope to full magnification we noticed one more detail: The bear wore a yellow tag in each ear. There were two possible explanations for the tags. She was one of Rick Mace's study animals. Or she was a nuisance bear relocated to the backcountry after learning to rummage through human food.

It was growing dark when I gave up on the stove and built a twig fire. After dinner, we carefully washed up, kicked apart the ashes, and found a whitebark pine snag from which to hang our food and cook gear beyond the reach of animals. Then Karen noticed something in the snow, directly under the pine tree. Bear tracks. Big ones. Fresh ones. Bear tracks don't last long in summer snow.

The loft of our sleeping bags offered protection from the night cold, but no protection from the night imagination. I pushed thoughts of the bear from my mind and closed my eyes. I was tired from our hike and all the fresh air and quickly fell asleep. But I snapped awake even quicker. I heard footsteps just outside the nylon tent wall.

Soft. Crunch. Crunch . . . crunch. I tried to imagine the sound into something besides paws on frozen snow, but could not. I felt Karen's fingers grab my arm. "Yeah," I whispered. "I hear it, too."

I cursed myself for ever reading that damn ranger's report from Glacier Park. ("It's got my arm off. . . . Oh God. I'm dead.") I unsheathed my can of pepper spray and popped off the orange safety tab. The potent compound is four hundred times stronger than the strongest jalapeño. You spray it into the nose of a bear to send it packing. Pepper spray has been documented effective in turning charges. I carry it in grizzly country because it is lighter and cheaper than a handgun and probably more effective. I pondered the effect of touching the can off inside the confines of a dome tent. Not good. A last-ditch effort.

We sat and listened for a time. Sometimes we could hear something. Sometimes, we could not. I thought of all the animals that had investigated my camps in the past: skunks, raccoons, porcupines, kangaroo rats, pack rats, ground squirrels, marmots, mountain goats, mule deer, elk, black bears. A moose once tripped over my guy line; a mountain lion once tried to eat my Lab puppy. On one hand, I thought, the sound could be made by any one of a dozen wild animals, most of them harmless. On the other hand, why not a hungry grizzly?

"It's probably the wind," I said.

"Does it sound like the wind to you?" Karen asked.

"Well . . . no."

Such thoughts are not conducive to restful slumber. The wind picked up. The woods were full of cracking branches and rustling boughs. The reaction was visceral and instinctive. Reason was locked in a closet in the basement of our minds. I could smell fear. That is not hyperbole. There was a distinct odor coming from the pores of our skin. I knew what a vicious dog smells when you shrink from it.

"This is ridiculous," I said, trying to sound braver than I felt. "We haven't even seen anything yet. It could be just the wind." I unzipped the tent and we peered outside. Karen held the flashlight, while I aimed the pepper spray. We saw nothing but darkness. No faint motion. No dim outline. No eyeballs reflecting red. Nothing. We stepped outside the tent, determined to settle this once and for all. The night wind chilled the sweat on our skin. We walked around the tent, probing the night with the flashlight. I shouted into the darkness: "Go on! Get out!"

The night offered no response. We looked at each other. We could either stand outside in our underwear or try to go back to sleep. Sleep never came, but dawn finally did. Sunlight turned gray to blue, prompting the chatter of a song sparrow. Groggy, I got up. I dressed and checked the snow and mud around the tent for spoor of whatever creature we had heard.

The only tracks I could find were left by mule deer. I hated to admit that our imagination had transformed a brown-eyed doe into a man-eater, but that was the evidence. The bear had done nothing to provoke my imagination but mind her business. For all we knew, she had never eaten anything more threatening than a glacier lily.

Karen and I broke camp. The stove was still on the blink, so we ate a cold breakfast. We staggered down the trail under the effects of sleep deprivation. Back in town, I called Rick Mace and asked if he knew of a large, adult bear wearing a pair of yellow plastic ear tags.

"That's number 96," Mace said, checking his files. "She is a female who is now twenty-two years old." Number 96 had raised several litters of cubs on the back side of Mount Aeneas, never troubling people. In fact, she was quintessentially shy. Humans, even Mace with his airplane and radiotelemetry gear, rarely caught a glimpse of her. I told Mace our story. I downplayed the part about sitting up all night.

"All right," Mace said. "You were lucky to see her. Maybe you ought to write about that one."

Chapter 4

The Land Wore One Robe

AMERICAN BISON
Bison bison

LEX BLOOD PADDLED FROM THE STERN OF THE CANOE, his mountain-weathered face appearing as if chipped from a block of hickory, dimples cut by the point of a knife. Judith Pressmar sat in the bow, a chin strap holding her brimmed hat aboard her head in the stout headwind. Between them arose a dromedary hump of gear—rubberized duffel bags, plastic ice chests, blue tarps and propane stove—as if the canoe had been hybridized with an Arabic camel.

As a college professor and man of habit, Lex talks in fifty-minute intervals, projecting his voice across the broad water as easily as across an auditorium. As a geologist, he speaks of time the way defense contractors speak of money: in vast, incomprehensible sums. On the subject of change, Lex takes the long view.

As Karen and I started backtracking the Lewis and Clark Trail, we confronted a problem. Our aim was to track down the creatures, plants, and phenomena that Lewis and Clark discovered nearly two centuries before. We wanted to learn how those species fared today. Our plan seemed simple enough. But we first got a sense of how much we had to learn at a place Lewis and Clark named Slaughter River.

That is where our canoes were heading. On today's map, Slaughter River is called Arrow Creek. Arrow Creek flows north across central Montana, seeping out of the Highwood Mountains, rippling slow and lackluster across flat rangelands, then slicing through the side canyons into the Missouri River. The name—Arrow—refers to a projectile in a native myth. Legend tells that a noble princess was tormented here by an evil suitor. Out of the blue, the sun launched an arrow, slaying the malefactor and setting the princess free. The Corps of Discovery arrived at Arrow Creek soaked and exhausted. The drone of flies filled their ears and the stench of death filled their nostrils. This was May 29, 1805. The Corps of Discovery's second year on the trail. The men struggled upstream, the river now leading due west. The side canyons of the Missouri were a crumble of soft shale and sandstone. Beyond that, the plain spread vast and treeless and alien. Stands of riverside cottonwood trees offered reprieve from the sun, but swarmed with mosquitoes and hid grizzly bears.

Every step of the way, the river tried to push the men back. Back to North Dakota. Back to St. Louis. Back all the way to the Gulf of Mexico. The Corps toiled miserably. The captains walked ashore. The enlisted men waded to their armpits, towing their pirogues behind them. They pulled their tonnage against the current, bare feet slipping for purchase in muddy slime or ankles twisting between sharp rocks. Leather towlines stretched and rotted and finally snapped.

On this afternoon, they came to a sandstone escarpment and the mouth of a small river. Lewis and Clark named this stream the Slaughter River for the gruesome scene they witnessed here. Running high with spring runoff, the Missouri River had dumped scores of bloated bison carcasses to rot on the bank. Lewis estimated at least one hundred bison were scattered here, creating "a most horrid stench." The corpses were naked and pale, and scavenging birds and animals made off slowly, bellies distended. It was a colossal scene of death. Yet it was a scene of prodigious life. It was a scene of bison.

NEARLY TWO CENTURIES LATER, our four canoes were on the same murky waters of the Missouri, mounded high with gear. Again it was late May. We were en route to Arrow Creek. To see what had changed. Our expedition took the leisurely route, floating downstream. We were eight boaters in four canoes. Besides Lex and Judith, they included John and Kris Bruninga, amateur fossil hunters so successful they are often given credit in publications written by professionals. Also along were my parents, celebrating their recent retirement with their first overnight canoe trip.

This White Cliffs section of the Missouri River is an official Wild and Scenic River, protected by federal law since 1976. Hundreds of visitors visit this 149-mile stretch every summer, squeezing a Lewis-and-Clark experience into a one-week camp-out. Local chambers of commerce and tourist handbooks tout the White Cliffs as the most pristine portion of the 8,000-mile Lewis and Clark Trail. But when one travels with a geologist and historian, the world takes a different slant. How unchanged this place is depends entirely upon how closely you care to look.

The world, as Lex sees it, exists in layers. A veneer of soil, sand, and sediment, pressed into rock. Each layer is laid down, younger atop the older, following a natural law as immutable as gravity. The Earth's crust is a giant calendar, read from the present surface down the staircase of strata. Sometimes the layers are upthrust and folded, sometimes shot through with intrusions, sometimes scoured, blown, or scraped away. But in the end, most often, sediments are set down in convenient, orderly layers.

Our canoes passed crumbling exoskeletons of homestead cabins. Judith told us these hardscrabble farms were built on the flat bends along the river during the land boom of the early 1900s. The boom that went bust when the land proved too dry to farm. Grass grew from the collapsed roofs. Sun-bleached rags hung from curtain rods, the air too dry for the fabric to rot. The empty homes seemed like tombstones to buried dreams.

At a lunch break, we climbed a bluff for a better view of the river. John found five stone rings, each thirty feet across. They were tepee rings marking the parameters of the lodges of a past family of buffalo hunters. The size indicated the lodges were erected after the Indians obtained horses around 1720. Indians, probably Blackfeet, erected their tents on the same bluffs each year, using the stones in lieu of tent pegs. In the center was the slight depression of the fire pit. On the east edge was the gap where the door met the morning sun.

Time. Time. To me, the prairie seems as ancient as it does immense. But this uppermost layer represents just a twitch of time that is the present.

LEX OFFERED A BRIEF HISTORY: A hundred million years ago, a shallow saltwater sea covered these plains. Layers of sediment settled at the bottom of the sea—layers which today are the strata of sandstone on the canyon walls. Dinosaurs roamed the seashore, until knocked off by a meteor some 65 million years ago. The sea went away. A parade of oddball mammals took the stage, including prototypical lions, camels, and horses. Only a couple million years ago, the earth's temperature dipped during the Pleistocene. The polar ice caps built up, dropping ocean levels until Asia fused with Alaska. The lions, camels, and horses left. Asiatic mammoths, oversize bears, and dire wolves took over North America. And, significantly, a large, shaggy, ox-like beast, *Bison priscus,* also arrived. *B. priscus* was huge beyond any bovine known today, with horns spanning six feet. This breed split into another large bison species, *B. latifrons,* and these two superbison breeds shared North America for 300,000 years.

Humans, also from Asia, came much later, perhaps 12,500 years ago. They pursued mammoths, initially, but when those elephants died out, North Americans turned to bison. Bison-hunting people exploited cliff traps called *pishkuns.* The word comes from the Piegan language and means *deep blood kettle.* Working in tightly organized, communal groups, these nomads staged great bison stampedes. With careful planning and stealthful execution, they surrounded entire bison herds. Once the bison moved to a favorable position, the hunters sparked a panic that sent the animals rushing over the cliff. Animals tumbled to their deaths by the hundreds. Tons of meat, bones, and guts, crumpled at the foot of the cliff. Bison that did not die in the fall were finished off with spears, clubs or, later, arrows. No bison were allowed to escape, since any survivor would remember the cliff and warn future herds away from it. Human survival demanded a certain ruthlessness.

Hundreds of pishkuns are scattered across the northern plains. The bottoms of these cliffs are strewn with layers of bison bones. Some pishkuns contain thousands of years of bones packed several meters deep, representing the deaths of hundreds of thousands of bison. Like the earth's sediments, the bones are stratified. The deeper one digs, the older the bones. The more stories they have to tell.

WE PADDLED TWO TO A BOAT. Karen, in a show of heroism, shared a canoe with her father-in-law. I paddled another boat, with my mother in the bow of our boat. Previous to this trip, her life included about twenty minutes in a canoe, decades before I was born. Still, the hours passed pleasantly and my mother was getting the hang of the basic paddle strokes.

Later in the afternoon, headwinds kicked in. Whitecapped waves blew directly upstream. "We should stick together in this wind," I called out. All shouted their agreement.

Waves crashed over our bow, thoroughly drenching poor Mom. River water sloshed around the floor of the canoe. The afternoon wasn't so warm that the water felt good. Moreover, the wind threatened to turn our boat sideways to the waves, which would have resulted in a cold swim, and soggy gear. I wrestled my paddle to keep the bow pointed downstream. The other canoes hugged the left bank, but I somehow pointed our bow too far out. The river was about a quarter-mile across and before I knew it we were in midstream, with whitecaps all around. The canoe bucked and rocked, each wave dousing my mother. The other canoes became teeny objects on the far bank.

"I thought we wanted to stick together," Mom shouted over the wind.

"Never mind," I shouted back. "Did I show you how to bail?"

With evening, the wind died down. The eight of us camped at Eagle Creek, across the Missouri from a three-hundred-foot cliff of sheer, white sandstone. When we arrived in late afternoon, the low light made the cliff shine like alabaster. The tint changed with the cant of the sun, the face glowing tangerine in the evening light and then lavender toward sunset. We pulled our canoes ashore, extracted packs of gear and hauled them to high ground. Nearly two hundred years before, the Lewis and Clark Expedition had done the same thing, at the same spot. Lewis described it as a "scene of visionary enchantment." That, at least, remained so.

Soon after our arrival at Eagle Creek my father noticed three black dots halfway down the face of the escarpment across the river. At first I dismissed them as odd, dark boulders.

"Hey Ben," my father said. "Dig out your binoculars. Those black spots are moving."

I screwed the binoculars into focus and, indeed, the black dots shuffled slightly. They were Angus cows, doing a clumsy imitation of mountain goats. Too stupid to fear heights, the cows had wandered on a ledge until they found insufficient room to turn around. They were stranded. "Cliffed out," as park rangers say of tourists caught in a similar pinch. One misplaced hoof and a cow would become the world's largest water balloon, falling a couple hundred feet before bursting on the rocks below. The cows were in a pickle. But we were far below and clear across the river. There was nothing to do but watch.

Through the binoculars and Karen's telephoto lens, we noticed a band of ranch hands already set at solving this problem. They arrived in a dusty Ford pickup and a Caterpillar bulldozer. They drove the bulldozer precariously near the edge of the cliff and dug the blade into the ground as a brake. The cowhands stood on the edge of the cliff and tipped their hats back and looked down at the cows and shook their heads a little. They tied ropes and cables to the bulldozer and dropped them over the cliff.

One cowhand, probably a veterinarian, rappelled over the edge with a jab stick—a tranquilizer dart on a small pole—in hand. He reached the first stranded beast, assembled the dart, and stabbed a cow hindquarter (new meaning for the word *cowpoke*). The drug evidently was not designed to completely knock out the cow, but merely relax it. Many a veterinarian has been seriously hurt by cattle in the controlled environment of a barn or vet's clinic. If this cow tumbled the wrong way, the vet was going down with it. The man slipped a harness around the creature's midsection and buckled it. He hooked the cable to the trussed cow.

Above all this, the men in cowboy hats looked over the edge of the cliff like men staring down a well.

The cow wobbled. The man on the ledge gave the men above the thumbs up and stepped out of the way. The ranch hands passed the signal to the operator of the bulldozer. The machine backed away from the cliff. Everyone stepped clear. The cable straightened and strained. The cleats of the tractor tread dug into the earth. Dust billowed as the cable sliced into the cusp of the soft cliff.

A full-grown Angus weighs maybe fifteen-hundred pounds and is in no way built for dragging up cliffs. Slowly, the taut cable hoisted the beast up the face. The cow dangled like a slobbering plumb bob, rising slowly, a pendulum with legs. The Cat belched diesel smoke and pulled. In a cloud of dust and saliva, the cow emerged at the sage flat. The bulldozer kept pulling, then stopped. Once the cow was away from the edge, the men untied it and slapped and pulled it until the animal was on its feet.

The cow flicked its tail and staggered back toward the cliff, loyally returning to the rest of the herd still stuck a hundred feet below. The men raised their hands and shouted, turning the cow away from the cliff and back toward the flats.

The cowhands and the man with the jab stick repeated their effort. Four more times, cows were drugged and trussed. One by one, the bulldozer hoisted the cows off the cliff. Each time, it appeared the cow might slip and tumble. But when the last cow was safe, the man with the jab stick climbed back up, too, and slapped dust off himself. Without so much as shaking hands, the men climbed aboard the bulldozer and the pickup truck and headed off.

We cheered. Once, people drove bison off these cliffs. Now, we drag cows up them. Times change. Even here.

WE PITCHED TENTS in a grove of cottonwood at the mouth of Eagle Creek, where the Bureau of Land Management maintains a fire pit and an outhouse. At sundown, Lex walked to the outhouse. It was a brand new crapper, the fancy kind with a solar panel over the vault and vent pipes and all. Didn't smell hardly at all.

Intent on the task at hand, his pants around his ankles, Lex looked up from the can to see a small motion in the corner of the outhouse. His eyes adjusted to the dim light. He saw a forked tongue test the air. Little buzzer of a tail. Rattlesnake. Prairie species. *Crotalus viridus.* First scientific specimen collected on June 15, 1805, along the banks of the Missouri River, presumably under more comfortable circumstances, by Meriwether Lewis.

Lex, a cool customer, finished what he had started. He stood up, slowly pulled up his pants and reached his long, skinny arm for the door. In one exaggerated step, he exited. Back at the campfire, he told us all about the snake.

That night in our tent, I awoke and knew I couldn't wait for dawn. By headlamp, I walked to the outhouse and opened the door. The little circle of yellow light probed the corners of the john. I didn't sit until I was sure the little serpent was absent. The bobbing circle of light from my forehead focused on a scrawl of graffiti on the clean, white outhouse wall:

"5/31/05. Lewis and Clark wuz here."

THE NEXT MORNING, we continued downstream. White pelicans rested on the river, launching skyward on their black-tipped wings as we approached. We left the alabaster white cliffs behind. The river took us past black towers of igneous rock—remains of extinct volcanoes that looked like castles from deserted kingdoms. We elected to camp near the castle called Dark Butte.

We beached, hauled our gear ashore, and piled it under a cottonwood tree. We all looked for flat spots, large enough for tents but devoid of cow shit. This is no simple task along Montana rivers. I tried to imagine the cow flops were buffalo chips, but couldn't quite make the stretch. When I finally found a spot, I returned to the pile of gear and picked up our tent. A four-foot-long bull snake wriggled across my feet. I yelped and everyone turned to see me hop backward about six feet.

"Just a bull snake," John said, scooping the serpent into his hands. "It'll keep the mice away." It coiled around his forearm. We held a quick vote and relocated the snake beyond camp.

That evening, Dad heard a faint whine from a tree near his tent. The source was a cub raccoon the size of a small guinea pig. The cub had fallen out of its den in a hollow tree and its mother evidently was too cautious to rescue it in daylight. Dad called us to look at the cub. It was cute, with blue eyes in its black mask. We took another vote and Dad picked the raccoon up by the scruff of its neck and deposited it back in the hole in the tree, to save it from the bull snake.

ANOTHER MORNING, another cup of coffee, and we were off again. After a morning paddle, we nooned at the former Slaughter River, across the broad Missouri from the mouth of Arrow Creek. We pulled our boats ashore, knotting the bow lines to the exposed roots of a cottonwood tree. We sat on the bank and unsacked our lunches. It was a warm spring day but we wore hats and long sleeves against the sun and mosquitoes. I flopped on my back and watched the treetops, the birds berserk with sundry spring urges. I chewed on a piece of grass and felt contentedness seep through my veins. My eyes drooped shut.

Discoveries often simply arrive, a seed falling on fertile soil like an apple dropping on Newton's noggin. Discovery is a matter of having your brain trained, your eyes open, and your wits about you. Of asking that ever-prudent question: What *is* that? Our discovery at Arrow Creek came poking up from the ground, while I snoozed in the sun.

It was Kris who discovered the bone. A small flake of white jutted out of the ground, partially exposed by river erosion. She dug it out of the dirt and rubbed the mud away with a thumbnail. The bone filled the palm of her hand. The sides were grooved and the top edge was serrated, but worn. It was a tooth of a bison. Teeth are harder than bone and will remain long after bone is decayed. "Hey," Kris said. "Look at this."

We had no way of telling how long this tooth had been buried in the soft bank before the water exposed it. A couple centuries was our guess. At this stream where the expedition had found the putrid bison carcasses, Lewis assumed they had stumbled across a pishkun and wrote a lengthy journal entry explaining the hunting technique. But experts today believe the animals were not driven over the cliff to their death, but rather had drowned earlier in the winter and been flushed downstream. The explorers noted wolves, belly-swollen from the feast, lolling among the dead bison. Eagles and vultures scavenged among the foxes and coyotes, turning the bisons' misfortune into their own fortune. Turning death back to life. Even the stench of death—the bacteria that stinks so—is the smell of a living microscopic organism. That's the weave of nature's fabric: the warp of life and the woof of death.

Kris's discovery was rich with possibility: that this bone was from one of the bison of the Slaughter River. At least, the tooth was a remnant of one of uncounted thousands of bison that had washed upon this riverbank for centuries. It was a moving and unusual moment, when history was something palpable. Because history is not normally something you can hold in your hand. Rather, history is bold lines of supposition connecting faint dots of fact. Case in point is the history of the bison.

LEWIS AND CLARK did not "discover" the American bison. Not even close. Early European explorers of the Atlantic Coast, the Florida Everglades, and the Mississippi River all saw bison. In the mid-1600s, bison were shot in the swamp that became Washington, D.C. Jefferson probably saw them in his boyhood at Monticello. The last bison in Pennsylvania was shot in 1801, two years before the Louisiana Purchase. Bison were among the first animals expelled by civilization.

To discuss this idea of what Lewis and Clark did or did not discover, though, is to unravel a ball of snakes that is this verb *discover*. In science, a creature is discovered when it is measured, weighed, and otherwise described in scientific literature. Historians credit Lewis and Clark with discovering three hundred species or subspecies of plants and animals. That is one perspective—and the one you get from history books, museums, and interpretive centers. But from another perspective, Lewis and Clark didn't discover a damn thing.

Every plant Lewis carefully pressed for Jefferson's herbarium, every animal Clark skinned for the American Philosophical Society archives, was known intimately by the native people of North America. Certainly that was true of the Great Plains bison. A Lakota father or Arikara mother lived in a home of bison, wore clothes of bison, ate the protein of bison. They knew bison in ways western science never could.

But discovery is whittled from the block of culture. In American scientific thought, Lewis and Clark were blazing trail. The Canadian fur-trappers were exploring, but with a mind toward commerce. The Spaniards had probed the American Southwest, but their primary motivations were gold and God. Because of their benefactor, Thomas Jefferson, Lewis and Clark went afield with at least a minimal grasp of scientific method. They saw things that few whites had seen before, but more importantly they described them with some sense of objective rigor. And that is the definition of *discover* I depend upon for this book, with apologies to other cultures and visions. The definition is by no means perfect. The Spaniards, the French, the English, and Native Americans were also discoverers. But we have to draw lines somewhere, if only for the sake of convenience.

The Corps's scouts saw bison near the site of present-day Kansas City, Missouri, in the first weeks of their journey. First they saw a few scattered individuals and then small herds. In August 1804 the party enjoyed its first bison roast near the southern edge of South Dakota. Neither Lewis nor Clark had ever seen one, but they knew exactly what it was and what it was good for. But the explorers were unprepared for what was to come: the vast herds that cloaked the Great Plains. This was perhaps the greatest concentration of large mammals that ever graced Planet Earth. And Lewis and Clark wrote the first scientific record. Many creatures that Lewis and Clark encountered taxed their descriptive abilities, but the multitude of wildlife overwhelmed them. The plains were filled not only with thousands upon thousands of bison, but similar herds of elk, and even larger numbers of pronghorn. The prey fed hosts of wolves and grizzly bears. It was a scene I can barely comprehend—and that scientists are still trying to puzzle together.

The classic view of American history is that Lewis and Clark shot their way across the Garden of Eden, that the land and fauna of interior North America was essentially virgin. Pristine. In this view, American Indians are perceived as noble innocents, taking from the land but only in harmonious ways, without adverse influence upon the overall scheme. North America is painted as paradise unaltered by human hands. In particular, the teeming herds of buffalo symbolize that phenomenon. This is a rich, strongly held idea. Part of me believes it still. But it is a view that, in all likelihood, is quite mistaken. At least, it is overly simplistic. The reality, as much as we can know it, is much more complicated.

LIKE ALL SCIENTISTS, Lewis and Clark faced the problem of quantification—how to count all these creatures. The bison herds grew larger and larger as the men progressed up the Missouri. The explorers grew increasingly flabbergasted. At first, a herd of three thousand bison was something shocking. A few weeks later, such herds were hardly worth a journal entry. As the bison grew in number, they became less and less wary. Soldiers passed in easy rifle range, finding the animals almost as docile as dairy cows. Curious bison followed the men for miles. Once, an orphan calf latched on to Lewis and followed him as if the captain were the animal's mother.

During the August rutting season, bison bulls bellowed around the camps, keeping the explorers awake all night. One rut-mad bull stampeded through camp; one enraged bull smashed a rifle belonging to Clark's slave, York. It was a small loss, consider-ing that the bison had almost crushed the heads of the sleeping men. In northeastern Montana, near the Milk River, the Corps had to beat bison out of their way with rocks and sticks. On Clark's float down the Yellowstone River, his crew was forced to wait for half an hour as a herd thundered across the river. Their journals snap and pop with words of astonishment.

In southern South Dakota, Lewis wrote: "The scenery, already rich, pleasing and beautiful, was still further heightened by the immense herds of Buffaloe."

In North Dakota, Lewis wrote: "Game is still very abundant. We can scarcely cast our eyes in any direction without percieving deer, Elk, buffaloe or Antelopes." And again at the mouth of the Marias River, in Montana: "The country in every direction around us was one vast plain in which innumerable herds of Buffalow were seen. . . ."

Upstream, near Great Falls, Lewis estimated that there were ten thousand bison within a two-mile radius of where he stood. At another point, he estimated being surrounded by twice that many.

"The whol face of the country was covered with herds of Buffaloe, elk and antelope," Clark wrote near the mouth of the

Yellowstone, on the western border of what is now North Dakota. Along the Yellowstone River, Clark pledged not to waste more ink estimating wildlife numbers, since he figured no one would believe him anyway.

Bison lived not only in the plains, but well into the Rockies. The Corps found bison sign near the Bitterroots, near the present border of Idaho. Small bands grazed the high alpine meadows well above timberline along the Rocky Mountain Front. But bison were not found everywhere in equal numbers. The herds were thin near the Mandan villages and other places where Indians gathered for long periods. During winter at these villages, native hunters performed long ceremonies to attract bison. The tribal men thought it would be useful if the powerful strangers of the Corps of Discovery would have sex with their wives, believing such an act would help attract buffalo. The young soldiers were happy to oblige. Sure enough, the bison showed up.

Bison were great wanderers, depleting one pasture, then rumbling hundreds of miles to find better grass. In some places, only brittle spoor and old bones indicated where the great herds had passed. Clark speculated that bison were more common in zones between territories of warring Indian tribes. It seems these demilitarized zones formed a sanctuary for the herds.

After the Lewis and Clark Expedition was complete, subsequent explorers rushed to fill in the remaining blank spots on the map of North America. Before striking out, they scoured the journals of Lewis and Clark, the logs kept by the expedition's sergeants, and any other sources of information. Initially, they sometimes suspected the captains had exaggerated a tad, especially when they described the numbers of bison. But when these doubters returned from their journeys and wrote their own journals, they said that, if anything, Lewis and Clark underestimated the number of bison. Explorers found bison from the desert of Chihuahua to the frigid interior of Canada. One Army colonel riding along the Arkansas River recorded a herd twenty-five miles long and fifty miles wide. "It was as if the land," he wrote, "wore a single robe."

When Thomas Jefferson sent Lewis and Clark out, the very idea of extinction was brand new. A few European intellectuals believed species could go extinct, and this idea shocked the western world. Jefferson stuck to the traditional, biblical view that creatures, once on earth, existed indefinitely. The nineteenth century proved Jefferson wrong. Species that were common for Lewis and Clark—passenger pigeons and Carolina parakeets, for examples—went extinct under habitat destruction and wanton gunning. The killing technology of the Civil War and the completion of the railroads very nearly demolished the bison. The entire process, from tens of millions of bison to only three hundred breeding-age adults, took just fifteen years, from 1868 to 1883.

In the traditional view of the American wilderness, the teeming herds found by Lewis and Clark were as timeless as the plains themselves. For years, historians and biologists assumed that before Indians obtained horses, aboriginal hunting was far too puny an effort to affect the bison. We could not imagine that nomads, on foot and armed with spears, could impact such an unbounded resource. But today, scholars such as Canadian ecologist Valerius Geist are challenging this view. They assert that the bison herds of 1800 were by no means "natural." To back up this claim, they point to the bison itself.

Let's roll the clock back to the Pleistocene. Recall that two species of bison, both much larger than today's version, roamed the continent for 300,000 years. These prototypical bison were shaped by incessant pursuit by dire wolves, enormous short-faced bears, and other giant bison-eaters. To survive, bison had to excel both at combat and at footraces. Natural selection built these antique bison to run fast and early, but also gave them great bulk and sweeping horns to stand their ground.

Human hunters entered North America at least 12,500 years ago and perhaps long before. The new North Americans changed the continent not only by hunting, but also by burning. As they roamed, they set the land afire to clear forests for easy walking and to regenerate grass fields to attract game. Fire is to the advantage of certain species and the bane of others. Just what effect people had on Pleistocene wildlife has been debated for decades. Fossils indicate that within 1,000 years of the arrival of humans, 70 percent of the large mammals of North America disappeared. Giant ground sloths. Mammoths. Beavers the size of black bears. Their fossils vanish just as the first clues of humans emerge. Compared to the usual ebb and flow of extinction and evolution, this seems unusually swift. One explanation is that human hunting pressure drove the mammoth and its peers to extinction. Just as spear-armed Maori exterminated the giant, flightless birds of New Zealand, the Asiatic immigrants hunted out the large animals of North America.

At any rate, about 22,000 years ago, early bison, *B. latifrons,* went extinct. About 10,000 years ago, another oversize proto-bison, *B. antiquus,* died out. Another bison, *B. occidentalis,* smaller than either *B. latifrons* or *B. antiquus,* emerged in the fossil record. *B. occidentalis* was a grazer who thrived in freshly burned grasslands.

Geist believes humans shaped bison into the animal they are today. The antique bison were massive, long-horned creatures, adapted to stand their ground against predators. Paleo-Indians could goad these defensive bovines into taking a stand and then slay them with spears. The bison that survived were the ones that elected to flee instead of fight. This led to a compact creature with stubby horns and swift legs, one-third smaller than its predecessors. This smaller breed, technically *Bison bison,* is the modern bison. The new kid on the evolutionary block, the American bison came into being only 4,000 years ago.

Since the last ice age, Geist argues, the incessant hunger of human beings sharply limited the range and numbers of bison. Bison numbers rose and fell with harsh winters, droughts, and moist periods, but were trimmed by the constant pressure of human hunting. This went on for thousands of years. Humans were such efficient hunters that they may have eliminated bison from the Columbia River basin and the Pacific Northwest long before Lewis and Clark.

In the 1400s, European sailors visited North America, seeking spices in the West Indies and cod off Newfoundland. Sailors introduced smallpox, typhoid, and other maladies to America, new diseases devastating to Native Americans. By 1600—the era of the Pilgrims at Plymouth Rock—disease had ravaged native people. Aboriginal numbers were reduced by millions across the continent. The result was not only a human catastrophe, but an ecological convulsion. Geist maintains that human pandemics suddenly lifted the predatory pressure off the bison. With millions fewer people killing and eating them, bison numbers exploded. Wolves and grizzlies had little effect. Bison expanded until tens of millions cloaked the prairie. There were more bison than the continent had ever seen. Upon this land came Lewis and Clark. Not a virgin wilderness, but one point in a long, unfolding story. A story always changing.

◈

IN THE LATE 1800S, a young cowboy named Theodore Roosevelt interviewed an elder herdsman. The old trailhand had ridden from Montana to North Dakota during the peak of the bison slaughters. He told Roosevelt that for hundreds of miles, he was never out of sight of a dead bison and never in sight of a live one. By the late 1880s, tons of wind-dried bison bones were stacked in great pyramids and ground into fertilizer. Even the bone deposits in ancient pishkuns were mined and powdered. A few harried, scattered bands of bison roamed the U.S.-Canada border, too small in such a vast land to be finished off. Elk, pronghorn, even whitetail deer, were reduced from millions to tens of thousands.

If Americans were ruthless and innovative in destroying their wildlife, they were also innovative and dedicated restoring it. Theodore Roosevelt, George Bird Grinnell, and others created a conservation system that was both original and effective. The system is built on three pillars: public ownership of wildlife, protection of key habitat, and reasonable restrictions on the killing of game animals. Thanks to this system, a million elk roam today's American West, along with a similar number of pronghorn. While these creatures are not nearly as abundant as in Lewis and Clark's day, Americans can enjoy them with little effort and expense.

Bison were America's first charismatic endangered species. Saving the bison was a cause célèbre of 1900, as saving gray whales was in the 1960s and saving harp seals was in the 1980s. The heroes of this story are not only the standard conservation celebrities like Roosevelt. They include unsung, independent folks like the Salish Indian Michel Pablo and Pend O'reille Indian Sam

Walking Coyote, who rounded up a band of orphan bison calves in southern Canada and herded them back to the United States. They raised a herd several hundred strong and shipped breeding stock to other private and public herds.

To save bison, we treated them like cattle. Bison were herded, fenced, branded, bred, doctored, inoculated, and culled.

Simultaneously we saved bison habitat, such as Yellowstone National Park, the National Bison Range in Montana, and Wood Bison National Park in Alberta. In Yellowstone, the U.S. Army tended its herd like cowboys guarding steers. (Don't miss the irony: This army called for the creature's extermination only decades before.) Captive bison increased. Today, North America has 250,000 bison, every one a direct descendant of those last 300 survivors. Nearly all of today's bison exist in private herds, raised for meat and profit. And if not profit, federal subsidy.

Wild bison, however, have not enjoyed the full benefits of these efforts. With bison, *wild* is relative. Wild animals are owned by the public, for public enjoyment over private profit. Wild animals select their own mates, exist alongside predators as much as possible, and are fenced as little as possible. As livestock, bison are plentiful. But as a free-roaming force of a wild prairie, bison are nearly extinct. Roughly 8,000 roam Yellowstone Park, the Niobara Preserve in Nebraska, and Custer Park, South Dakota. Yellowstone contains America's largest wild bison herd—about 4,000 head. Since Yellowstone bison harbor a cattle disease, they are confined behind a fence of bullets, shot dead if they cross park boundaries.

Today's bison are a crop. Inevitably, domestication results in a vapid version of the wild original, as it has for the genetically lobotomized cow, the oversized and underflavored strawberry, the Golden Delicious apple.

But bison are not domesticated. Not yet. Bison corrals are built of the same steel guardrails that keep trucks on highways. When an angry bull kicks at its corral, the leg flashes so fast you barely see the motion, until suddenly there is the slam of hoof against steel and the resulting dent. A wild heart still beats in that cavernous chest.

KRIS SCRAPED A THUMBNAIL against the cracked enamel of the bison tooth. She passed the object around our circle. We turned it in our fingers, feeling its heft. I felt the worn cusps, imagined the sound of grass ripping from prairie earth, the rhythmic motion of the jaw. I imagined the one-ton beast: fly-switch tail; snowplow of a head; dust rising from woolen flank; a cinnamon calf nosing an udder. I stretched to imagine a herd of a hundred, a thousand, a million. Ten million. Thirty million. And back to three hundred.

I am not sure of the lesson of Slaughter River. Perhaps simply that nothing began with Meriwether Lewis and William Clark. Nor with Christopher Columbus or Leif Erickson. Nor even with some forgotten nomad exploring the tundra now on the bottom of the Bering Strait.

Perhaps this is another lesson: We are capable of knocking things over and smashing them before we realize what we are doing. And that is reason enough to proceed with caution.

Chapter 5

Darkness and Luck

MISSOURI RIVER BEAVER
Castor canadensis missouriensis

KAREN AND I CARRIED OUR MAD RIVER CANOE UPSIDE
down, ashwood gunnels riding our
shoulders. The boat is sixteen feet long
and green and I imagine we looked like
members of some tribe of vegetarians,
returning home after paddling to death a

gargantuan zucchini. Our sockless sneakers padded down the dirt path. At river's edge, we counted to three, gave a shrug, and rolled the boat onto the Madison River. Once afloat, the canoe tugged downstream as if by its own will. The canoe once transported people across distance. In a world of supersonic jets and space shuttles, the canoe now transports across time.

This broad, high valley in southwestern Montana was buffed and polished by the evening light. The timbered heights of the Bridger Range glowed on the eastern horizon, the Tobacco Root Mountains rising dark in the west. Cars roared over the Interstate 90 bridge behind us. The low July sun electrified the water. Swallows—little mosquito falcons—raced through the sky, taunting any creature conceited enough to think itself graceful.

Our camp was pitched at Headwaters State Park near Three Forks, Montana. Here, three great rivers of Montana, the Jefferson, Madison, and Gallatin, converge into one. This is the starting gate for the Missouri River, the longest in the United States. From Three Forks, it's 2,565 miles to the Missouri's mouth near St. Louis. Downhill all the way.

Members of the Lewis and Clark Expedition were the first European Americans to visit this spot, spending two days here in late July 1805. The captains knew the art of flattery and named the rivers for their commander in chief, President Thomas Jefferson, their secretary of state, James Madison, and their secretary of treasury, Albert Gallatin.

Our boat was on the Madison. Somewhere downstream from us, hidden in a maze of willow and water, was the mouth of the Jefferson River and the technical source of the Missouri. Even farther downstream, near Lewis Rock, our bicycles were hidden in a patch of riverside brush. This was near the mouth of the

Gallatin. Our odometer told us it was five miles to our cached bicycles by the road. We weren't sure how far it was by way of the river.

Madison, the man, is famous for writing the U.S. Constitution. But Madison, the river, is famous for its trout. The river flows clear and clean, but dense with aquatic vegetation. It offers up great blizzards of summer insects: caddis flies, salmon flies, mayflies, even an aquatic form of butterfly. These insects in turn support one of the greatest densities of trout in any North American stream.

In season, the Madison is lined with chic fly-fishers. They pay thousands of dollars to hook the river's legendary brown and rainbow trout (also thoroughly exotic and unnatural). But this evening, a young man and woman fished the Madison in the shadow of the overpass, wearing jeans and black rock-concert T-shirts. Their fishing gear consisted of a single spinning rod, a bobber the size of a hardball, and a juicy nightcrawler.

"You sure we have time for this?" Karen asked. Voice of reason. The day was tired, the sun drooping toward its westward station. I was losing my knack for time. I had packed away my watch. The pale swath on my wrist had tanned a uniform brown.

"Yeah," I said, squinting into the sunset. We had been in the hot car all day. The promise of a cool evening float was irresistible.

"I think we have time. It will be refreshing. A quick evening paddle to lift the spirit. What's the worst that could happen?"

"Drowning," Karen said. "We could drown. That would be the worst."

Sorry I asked. When Karen and I dated, we often kayaked together on the rivers near our home. At the end of one outing, when we were tired and sloppy, the current caught Karen's boat, flipped her upside down, and swept her under a downed tree. The deadliest thing on the river.

I watched helplessly—too far away to reach her. She tried to roll upright against the force of the branches, but they shoved her back under. I saw her helmet break the surface, her mouth snatch a lungful of air, before she disappeared underwater. Finally, her helmet bobbed back to the surface. Karen slipped out of the boat and swam sidestroke to shore. All she lost was an expensive graphite paddle. But the lesson was learned: Take these rivers seriously. Events do not always play out as you might expect.

Take this particular point in geography, for example. Three Forks. The Corps of Discovery saw this place of great opportunity. This is where they were going to get rich. Instead, Three Forks became a place of horror, bloodshed, and death. Events don't always play out the way you expect.

"I think it will be OK," I said.

"Yeah," Karen said. "Let's paddle."

NATIVES OF NORTH AMERICA crafted a variety of canoes. The Algonquin used birch bark. The Inuit paddled umiaks of whalebone and sealskin. The Arikara made circular bull boats of buffalo hides stretched over willow frames. The Kootenai wove canoes of cedar bark. The first people of Hawaii arrived in canoes lashed together with coconut-frond ropes, following the stars. The Nootka and other tribes of the Pacific Northwest carved entire cedar logs into swift and ornate war canoes, from which they harpooned gray whales.

Lewis and Clark paddled the most primitive canoe: the

dugout. They chiseled out cottonwood logs on the Missouri and Yellowstone Rivers. On the Clearwater River, the Nez Perce showed them how to burn out the heartwood of ponderosa pine logs. The logs tended to crack and take on water, becoming heavy and unresponsive.

The Corps was particularly taken with the boats and paddling skill of the Clatsop and Chinook people of coastal Washington and Oregon. After their winter at the mouth of the Columbia, when it was time to return home, the Corps tried to buy a canoe from their native neighbors. But the Clatsop weren't selling cheap and the Corps had little to offer. Lewis solved this problem by ordering his men to steal the boat. The Fort Clatsop canoe larceny has vexed historians, who consider the incident the one great flaw in Lewis's shining record of honor.

Lewis would have coveted our sixteen-foot Mad River Explorer. The Explorer was our first purchase after we were married, the boat somehow symbolic of our new partnership. Like our partnership, the boat is resilient, but requires a bit of maintenance. The hull is scraped and dented, but remains sound.

Some people call canoes "divorce boats." And not without reason. Once you take off on a canoe trip, no matter how brief, you are no longer an individual. Your fate depends entirely on your ability to communicate well and to make and execute sound decisions together. Many relationships disintegrate under this stress. Karen and I follow a few basic rules and our paddling partnership has held, through placid water and rough.

Rule One: Never do a fool thing like paddle a river without first scouting it.

Rule Two: Never do a fool thing like paddle a river you have never scouted, if it's about to get dark.

But Three Forks was simply too much to resist.

Rule Three: Never obey all the rules. Karen took the bow. I put my left sneaker on the floor of the canoe and kicked off the bank with the right. I glanced at the setting sun, gave the paddle a pull and a twist, and pointed the bow downstream.

LEWIS AND CLARK arrived at Three Forks the hard way, hauling their dugouts upstream. Reaching the source of the Missouri was a major milestone. They might have celebrated longer, but the expedition was fraught with illness. The peaks around them reached ten thousand feet above sea level. Much stood between them and the Pacific.

Aside from its geographic importance, the Corps noted something else about Three Forks: beavers. The place was infested with them. Beaver dams and floodwaters gave them fits. But this abundance also had its advantages.

"I think the tale a most delicious morsal," Lewis wrote of North America's largest rodent. "When boiled, it . . . is sufficiently large to afford a plentiful meal for two men."

The beaver has other uses for its great paddle-blade of a tail. For one thing, beavers swim with their tails, sculling with the broad face. The tail also is a signal: A slap on a calm water surface sounds like a warning shot. And in the beginning of the nineteenth century, there was plenty for a beaver to be nervous about.

The trade in beaver pelts predates Columbus. Beavers were eradicated from Great Britain by the thirteenth century and from much of Europe shortly thereafter. In 1664, when King Charles II granted a large chunk of North America to his brother, James,

King Charles charged rent in beaver pelts. When the Mayflower returned to England after dropping off the pilgrims at Plymouth Rock, its hold contained beaver pelts. By the mid-1700s, Canada's Hudson's Bay Company was exporting tens of thousands of beaver pelts annually. By the time of Lewis and Clark, beavers were virtually extinct east of the Mississippi.

The Corps was outfitted with steel traps, and members set them nightly. Beavers actually drew more blood of the Corps of Discovery than did grizzly bears. One evening, George Drouillard, the Corps's masterful half-Shawnee scout, killed two beavers and wounded a third. When he tried to finish off the wounded animal, the beaver laid open the man's knee with those tree-felling incisors. Beavers were even harder on Seaman, Lewis's dog. The Newfoundland splashed to retrieve a wounded beaver that turned and lacerated the dog's leg, nicking an artery. The dog survived, but only after some quick first aid.

Aside from their modest use for food and pelts, the Corps let the beavers alone. They could not afford to amass a large stash of pelts. So when the Corps entered Three Forks, it was like paddling through a stream of hundred-dollar bills, but being unable to snatch at them. The River of Unrequited Profit.

While camped at Three Forks, Lewis and Clark faced another pressing decision. Days were growing short. The portage around the Great Falls had consumed their time and energy. The explorers had to find the Lemhi Shoshone, do some quick horse-trading, and get over the Rockies before the autumn snow. But which of these three rivers to follow? Which led to the homeland of the Lemhi? For that, they sought the advice of Sacagawea.

Three Forks was the home of Sacagawea's people, the Lemhi Shoshone. When Sacagawea was about twelve years old, her family was encamped at Three Forks and fell under attack by Haidatsu warriors. Most of Sacagawea's family was killed. She and another girl were taken captive. The strangers took the orphans back to their homeland, in the flatlands that are today North Dakota.

There, a French trader named Toussaint Charbonneau won the two girls on a bet. In 1804, four years after Sacagawea was captured at Three Forks, she and Charbonneau wintered at the Mandan village. Perhaps as young as fourteen, Sacagawea was pregnant with Charbonneau's son. At Fort Mandan, Charbonneau met Lewis and Clark and signed on as an interpreter to the expedition. Sacagawea and Clark's man, York, were the two slaves of the expedition.

Charbonneau was an unsavory character, who probably gave Sacagawea a disabling case of gonorrhea. One evening, Clark rebuked Charbonneau for beating Sacagawea. I imagine this was quite a beating, since Clark was a slaveowner himself and no stranger to brutality.

Sacagawea proved a greater asset to the expedition than Charbonneau. Sacagawea is fabled as a guide, but it was only near Three Forks that she recognized the land. Stoically she described the battle in which she was taken captive. She remembered a feature of the landscape: a broad escarpment of stone that, in the distance, looks like a swimming beaver. The valley is still called the Beaverhead.

TO FIND A SMALL BAND of Lemhi natives in this expansive land, Lewis took a few men and forged ahead of the main group. Lewis's squad hiked up the Jefferson River Valley and spread out across the sagebrush plain. Before long, the Jefferson River also branched into major tributaries. Here was another choice.

Lewis took the fork now known as the Big Hole River. Clark and the rest were coming up behind with their canoes and gear. Lewis did not want Clark to take the wrong fork, so he wrote a note, then stabbed it on a green willow in the middle of the river where Clark was sure to see it. Then he continued on.

Later, Clark and the rest pulled the laden canoes upstream. But Clark did not see the note. He took the wrong fork, just as Lewis had feared. Clark's men soon found themselves in a jungle of beaver dams and braided channels. When they tried to turn back, the dugout flipped and soaked the medical kit and other sensitive gear.

The dunking forced another costly delay to dry the supplies. Eventually the frustrated captains regrouped. Lewis asked why Clark had not followed the instructions on the note. What note? Clark responded. They puzzled over this until reaching the same conclusion: Something had chewed down the willow pole and taken the note with it. A beaver.

THE CANOE is a lovely, hypnotic mode of travel. At least when you're headed downstream. And if things aren't moving too fast. And if you have enough daylight to see.

We passed a beaver lodge—a modest, suburban model about three feet high. Beavers build their lodges by stacking sticks and mud together in a pile, either on a bank or in the middle of a pond. When the pile has reached a certain size, they burrow underwater, drilling a passageway under the sticks. The creatures then hollow out the center of the lodge into living quarters. Beavers seem to be annoyed by the sound of running water, genetically programmed to plug things up. The dams can be marvelous feats of engineering. The largest dam ever recorded in scientific literature was found just upstream from here on the Jefferson River. It was more than a half-mile long and sturdy enough to ride a horse across.

As we paddled, a great blue heron launched against the pinkening sky. "I love the way they do that," Karen said. "They just fold up those long legs, flap their wings once and are aloft."

An osprey—fish eagle—wheeled over a hidden oxbow. These rivers are all drawn down by irrigation, watering alfalfa to feed to cows and horses. This evening there was enough flow to keep us swiftly moving but not enough to completely cover the rocks and logs.

The source of the Missouri is not static. Like a child with a new box of crayons, the river cannot stay inside the lines. The rivers slip and slide with the spring floods. Channels are cut, moved, shunted back and forth across each other. Gravel bars pile up after each flood, then are dispensed and scattered with the next.

"We've got a choice here," Karen said. We quickly approached a split in the channel. "Which way do you want to go?"

I had no clue. These channels divided the river fifty-fifty. I flipped a coin in my head.

"Let's stay right," I said. I swept my paddle in a long, curved stroke and the canoe obediently pointed down the right-hand channel.

Immediately, this appeared to be a bad choice. The water was still finding its route, still determining the path of least resistance. We entered a snarl of fluid dynamics. The river channel dropped into one sharp bend and then another. The boat handled the turns, thanks mostly to its own design and not my attempts at steering. The water squeezed into a narrow space, flowing fast, then poured into another tight curve. Just looking at it, I knew this bend was too tight.

"Brace!" I shouted. A brace is a flat stroke across the surface of the water that steadies the boat. Karen braced, even though I shouted the command more to myself than to her. The canoe tipped precariously on one side.

"Brace!" I shouted again. My vocabulary was lodged in a one-word panic. The boat tipped. I threw the weight of my body on the high side of the boat. Water began to spill over the downside gunnel.

Karen arched her torso out of the boat, reached as far as she could and thrust her paddle straight down. With a tug, she pulled the blade toward her. An instant later, she vaulted the gunnel, splashed into the water, and grabbed the bow line and pulled to shore. The boat was anchored. I exhaled as she pulled the boat to shore.

As Karen held the bow line, I bailed water out of the boat with my baseball cap.

"That was close," she said. "I didn't know you were in a mood for a swim."

We weren't so far into the side channel that we couldn't wade out of this mess. We tipped the boat, spilled the water, then hoisted the canoe on our shoulders and carried it upstream. We walked to the main channel and set the boat down and resumed our places. I shivered from the cold water and the excitement. We took off again downstream.

Who said there are no second chances?

◈

In 1806, after wintering on the Pacific, Lewis and Clark returned to the Missouri River. They rushed back to St. Louis after more than two years in the wilderness. But in the final days of the journey, they happened across a pair of beaver trappers heading upstream.

One member of the Corps elected to leave the expedition, join the trappers, and stay in the wilderness. This was Pvt. John Colter, who thus joined the first wave of trappers to exploit the Missouri. Colter signed on with an adventurous Spaniard named Manuel Lisa. The next year, Colter explored what is now Yellowstone National Park. In 1808 and 1809, he trapped around the Shoshone River, in north-central Wyoming.

Lisa founded the Missouri River Fur Company, with principal investors including William Clark and Reuben Lewis, the brother of Meriwether Lewis. Shortly after Lewis and Clark's return, Lisa built a fort on the Bighorn River, a tributary of the Yellowstone, about two hundred miles east of Three Forks. Lisa hired three members of the Corps of Discovery as trappers: Colter, George Drouillard, and Pvt. John Potts. In 1808, they returned to trap at Three Forks. This development was a major shift in the balance of power in the central plains. The Blackfeet responded by terrorizing the newcomers.

Colter's Run has become a Western legend. There are a few different versions, but they boil down to this: Potts and Colter trapped as a pair, setting traps by night and collecting pelts each morning. One morning in 1810, they were trapping the Jefferson River by canoe when they heard the rumbling of hooves. Colter thought the sound was Indian ponies and suggested a retreat. Potts figured they had spooked a bison herd and goaded Colter to keep trapping.

Potts was wrong. The two men were soon met by perhaps five hundred Blackfeet. The tribesmen ordered the trappers to shore. Colter turned the boat to shore. Once within reach, an Indian seized Potts's rifle. Colter wrestled the gun back and passed it to Potts. Potts pushed the canoe back into the current. An Indian drew his bow and hit Potts with an arrow.

Potts responded by leveling his gun and shooting the Indian dead. The tribesmen riddled Potts with arrows and bullets, until his blood pooled in the bottom of his canoe. Then the Blackfeet dismembered Potts and rubbed his steaming heart in Colter's face.

The warriors took Colter back to their camp and debated what to do with him. Eventually they decided to have a bit of sport. They stripped Colter and let him go. They gave him a short head start and told him to run for his life.

Colter ran, naked and terrified. He headed straight for the river, six miles away. The prickly pear cacti ripped into his bare feet. But he kept running. His pulse pounded in his ears. Blood streamed out of his nostrils, down his beard, and over his chest. The Blackfeet raced for Colter. After five miles, one of the warriors closed in. About to be overtaken, Colter spun around to face the man.

The warrior had a spear, but muffed the throw. The lance broke when it hit the ground. Colter and the warrior wrestled for the weapon, each man clawing for his own life. Colter emerged with the sharp end of the weapon and ran the point through his opponent's chest. Colter stood and resumed his run.

Colter made it to the river by dusk, but the tribesmen were closing in. Colter jumped into the water and swam downstream, finally crawling into a logjam. He hid there all night shivering underwater while the Indians searched the shore. At dawn Colter pulled himself from the water and ran. He ran seven days to

Manuel Lisa's fort. Colter ran the equivalent of a marathon a day, for a week, running on rocky, cactus-strewn ground and across a mountain pass on the way. He arrived so bloody and battered that his partners failed to recognize him. But he was alive.

KAREN LIKES TO LEAD. Dancing. Paddling. Makes no difference. She sits in the bow, prying and drawing with her paddle blade. She gets bored if she must leave the steering to me.

After our initial mishap, the river took on a more forgiving mood. We followed the main channel as the evening faded. A pair of sandhill cranes stood on a sandbar. Their red-topped heads made them look like birds wearing berets. We stopped paddling, trying to appear like a log floating downriver. Sandhills are big, gawking birds. From their position on the sandbar, their eyes were higher than ours. As we passed, they looked down at us from only a few feet away. They did not startle as we passed.

It was as if someone had pulled the plug on the day and the sunlight was running down the drain. High clouds blocked any light from the stars or moon. I gave up trying to look downstream. I could see Karen, but not in detail. She shifted off the cane seat and knelt on the floor of the canoe. This is the pose that gets the center of gravity as low as possible. In a few moments, we would be paddling blind.

"Watch for logs or rocks," I said. "We don't want to hit anything."

"Don't get your hopes up," Karen said. "I can only see about ten feet in front of me."

When we did happen upon a rock or a submerged log, Karen

gave a little shout, telling me to pull left or right, and then dug her own paddle in. We slipped past each log, each rock, with only a slight nudge. Still, a canoe is a canoe. It doesn't always take much of a nudge to send one over. We floated on. Not really paddling. Just ready to respond.

When I first heard the noise, my head snapped around like it was jerked by an invisible hand.

Splash! A minor explosion leapt off the port side.

"Jeez," I said. "What was . . ."

Splash! Another explosion erupted off the starboard. I twisted to catch a glimpse of it. It was as if cannonballs were landing around us.

Splash! A third time.

"Beavers!" Karen said. "We're in the middle of a bunch of beavers." And a fourth *splash* sounded off, as if in punctuation.

Beavers work by night. Between the dark and our silence, we had interrupted a whole lodgeful of them. I glimpsed a beaver skimming across the dark smoothness of the river surface. Its back was glossy and wet. It struck me as both chubby and stream-lined. The beaver approached the bank and then turned like a swimmer at the edge of the pool. Before he disappeared, he cocked that big, flat tail and—*splash!*—slapped the water.

Then we were alone. In the dark. On the river. We had passed the point where the Madison flowed into the Jefferson. The Missouri River was fortified with two-thirds of its flow. The Gallatin waited for us somewhere downstream.

On top of this, we were constantly presented with side chan-nels and channels on side channels. Even in daylight, reading side channels is more of an art than a science. Now, we could only pick our route by the sound of running water and by gut hunch. We saw a distant light from a farmhouse, perched well away from the river. We were still wet, and the night wind made us shiver slightly under our life jackets. I paddled harder to keep warm.

AFTER POTTS'S DEATH and Colter's narrow escape, many of Lisa's men were too frightened to leave their fort. George Drouillard, himself half-Indian, taunted the other trappers. He bragged that he was too much of an Indian to be caught by the Indians.

The Blackfeet disproved this hypothesis. They caught Drouillard on the banks of the Jefferson. His fellow trappers found his corpse mutilated and beheaded, his entrails strewn across the sagebrush. The Blackfeet caught Drouillard on his horse. He dropped to one side, trying to keep the animal between himself and his assailants, turning the horse as the warriors circled him, firing arrows and bullets. Eventually the horse bled out and Drouillard had to crouch behind the carcass until he ran out of ammunition. The loss of Drouillard was a breaking point. Manuel Lisa was forced to abandon Three Forks.

But the Blackfeet could not hold back the trappers for long. Hundreds of mountain men spread across the West. Two great fur empires, the Rocky Mountain Fur Company and the American Fur Company, clashed over the new fur country. They combed the river bottoms, methodically trapping from the main rivers up to the dendritic headwaters. The idea was to catch all the beaver, before your competitor did.

No North American creatures except human beings cause such change to their habitat as do beavers. Their dams alter the flooding patterns of entire watersheds. Their reservoirs gradually fill in with soil, becoming willow flats and marshy bogs. These bogs are prime habitat for creatures from songbirds to moose. Remove the beaver, and you pull the underpinning from the whole works.

Thirty years after the Lewis and Clark Expedition, a scientifically minded explorer named Prince Maximilian came up the Missouri to Three Forks. He found the place devoid of beaver. From the main stem of the Missouri River to the mountain headwaters, the beavers were virtually gone.

THE LEWIS AND CLARK EXPEDITION was about commerce as much as it was about science. After the West was explored, it became the land of fur traders, then copper kings and timber and cattle barons. There is still money to be made in the West. The silicon capitalists settle the suburbs of Boise and Seattle. Old mansions are converted to bed-and-breakfast inns or the headquarters of county historical societies. New mansions sprout on the ski hills and lakeshores.

It's hard for me to imagine that trappers like John Colter headed West for money alone. The work was too difficult, too dangerous, for such a small return. Similarly, something more than economic opportunity connects us to today's West. Something beyond nostalgia and scenery. Many of us could make more money elsewhere, but we don't seriously consider moving. Television commercials tell us we should want more. Yet the promises from elsewhere are lost amid the crime, traffic, and pollution that seem worse everyplace else.

The landscape offers an attraction beyond the reach of the dollar. Our lives seem richer out here, no matter what the bank account says. Our lives seem to make more sense. We try not to measure the value of our lives by our stock portfolios. Instead we focus on the people we love, the communities we build, the battles we wage, the experiences we have.

The stage for such a life is a valuable thing—growing more valuable as it becomes increasingly rare. So every year the West grows more crowded. The map we once loved for its emptiness becomes scrawled with lines. The defining feature of the West—the glorious space—becomes less spacious. We slowly transform the Western landscape into an arid New Jersey, or an Ohio with topographic relief. We love the West. And the West breaks our hearts.

But I had little time for such thoughts. A troubling sound came from downstream.

In the dim light, Karen and I could see an escarpment ahead of us. We knew the rock was near the spot where we had cached our bicycles. The sound of the river, like the dim light, bounced off that rock. In the dark, the river sounded like a minor waterfall. The noise was magnified, no doubt. But how much? We could not tell.

We were nearing the mouth of the Gallatin River, which meant . . . what? Rocks. By the sound of it, yes. A beaver dam? Downed cottonwood trees? Perhaps. Disaster? Could be. Whatever it was, the current was pulling us right into it.

"I say we bail out," Karen said. "Running a rocky channel in the pitch black is not my idea of fun." Which brings up Happy Paddling Rule Number Four: Don't push your luck.

"OK," I said. "I'm with you."

We aimed the bow to shore and landed. We pulled the boat up on the bank, beyond the reach of the river, and anchored the bow line. We picked our way beyond the tangle of riparian brush. We emerged at the county road and jogged the last half-mile to our bicycles. The layer of clouds broke as I opened the bike lock. Starlight lit the empty road. We pedaled hard back to camp, the bicycles rocking beneath us, and the knobby tires singing against the tarmac. We were hungry as jackals and giddy from the released tension. We ate a hurried dinner, laughing at our little adventure. We returned the next morning for the boat.

IN 1810, John Colter left the wilderness. He took a wife and his pension and set to farming in Missouri. He claimed that Captain Lewis died owing him $377 in back pay and unsuccessfully sued Lewis's estate for it. The mountain man who had crossed the continent, explored Yellowstone, and outrun the Blackfeet died of jaundice in 1813 at age thirty-nine.

Even without Colter, Potts, and Drouillard, Manuel Lisa tried to continue at the fur trade. In 1823, Missouri River Fur Company crews suffered another massacre by the Blackfeet. Eventually the company was squeezed out by the American and Rocky Mountain fur companies and dissolved into a quagmire of lawsuits and counterclaims.

Sacagawea remained with Charbonneau after the expedition. Clark's journals indicate she died young, at about age twenty-two, in what is now South Dakota. But in the oral tradition of the Shoshone, Bird Woman left Charbonneau and roamed throughout the West, living some one hundred years. Two places claim Sacagawea's grave, one in South Dakota, the other in Wyoming.

The beavers survived the fur trade. Eventually silk replaced beaver fur as a millinery favorite. Conservation measures—specifically trapping limits and relocation efforts—were implemented. Beavers rebounded. Today, beavers thrive across the country. In Washington, D.C., within the shadow of the Jefferson Memorial, beavers waddle out of the tidal basin at night to chew down the city's prized cherry trees. Here at Three Forks, beavers are forever building dams, flooding the campground, washing out culverts.

Once again, the country abounds with beavers.

Chapter 6

Fishing with the Ghost of Silas Goodrich

WESTSLOPE
CUTTHROAT TROUT
Oncorhynchus clarki lewisi

CUTTHROAT TROUT LIVE SUSPENDED IN BEAUTY. THEY
breathe beauty, a million capillaries in
their gills pulling oxygen from it. If it's a
pond, brook, lake, or river that can host
wild cutthroat trout, it is a body of water
of utmost clarity and purity, with water

clear as molten glass. We are drawn to these waters the way we are drawn to a healthy human figure: by instinct. We know what does us good.

If the water loses its beauty, if it becomes tepid, murky, or stagnant, it may continue to host fish, perhaps even trout. But they will not be westslope cutthroat trout.

This said, on the scale of cutthroat trout waters, Griffin Creek is not much to look at. In fact, it is a pitiful, beleaguered brook in western Montana. Griffin Creek is about the width of a New York City sidewalk, but tumbles, spills, flows, and foams along its path. The water polishes the cobblestones round and smooth, flowing through a tunnel of underbrush. Two anglers would stumble all over each other, fishing its banks. This is a perfect stream to fish alone. Or fish with a ghost. A ghost by the name of Silas Goodrich.

I lowered myself down the steep bank, grabbing one tree trunk then another, the disassembled rod in my clenched teeth, brachiating like some kind of ape. My feet half-tumbled, loosing miniature landslides. Sharp little rocks filled my sneakers. When I reached the stream edge, I found myself looking over a waterfall that exploded into froth where water met rock. The forest was July-crisp, but the mist of the waterfall and the shade of the riparian forest chilled the air. I walked a safe distance upstream and stepped into the water. My ankles ached in the cold. The cold tells you: This is a cutthroat stream.

The world-record cutthroat trout weighed forty-one pounds and was pulled out of Pyramid Lake, Nevada, in 1925. Here in Montana, the record is a fifteen-pounder. The record cutthroat for Griffin Creek can only be measured in ounces. This is a modest stream, full of modest fish.

The stream was so clear I immediately spied a little trout lurking under the opposite cut bank. Silver flank. Spotted like a cheetah. The fish luxuriated in the dense green shade.

My rod was still in two pieces, my tackle in the little pouch around my neck. My eyes locked on target. Fish. Prey. Pray.

I kept my eyes on the fish as my fingertips connected the pieces of the rod and twisted the ferrule tight. Without looking, my fingers ran the line through the guides. I opened my creel, removed the little tackle box, and popped open the lid. I selected my smallest lure, like a dime with a treble hook. I tied the lure to the line with my favorite knot, the supergranny. I extracted my needle-nose pliers and snipped off two of the three hooks. I grasped the remaining hook by the point of the pliers and squeezed the barb flat.

I cocked the rod and fired the little lure into the shadow. It landed with a *plunk*. The trout darted across the stream, a silver arrow fired underwater. The fish zipped directly away from the lure. I reeled quickly, cocked the rod, and again flicked my wrist. I launched the little lure to the point just beyond the spot where the silver arrow had disappeared. The lure plunked again and I retrieved it. The lure arrived in the clear water at my feet, shining on the wet pebbles like a piece of misplaced jewelry. Untouched.

Trouble was, this was a tight spot from which to cast. Fir boughs drooped overhead. Willows crowded up behind, as if trying to read a newspaper over my shoulder. This angler needed a better angle.

So I stepped atop a river-sculpted rock that rose in a mossy shadow. I tilted my rod sidearm. I leaned toward the stream, feeling for purchase with the soles of my sneakers. I cocked my wrist back, took a steady aim, and my sneakers let go of the rock. As my lure flew through the air I collapsed off my perch. I stumbled, splashing and staggering, to remain upright. Gravity won. My bare shin caught another rock—a jagged little number that scraped a long, shallow wound. I felt the warm blood trickle before I even looked.

I stood in the water, inspecting the damage. The water dissolved the coagulants, so the red smeared vividly across my leg. Fishing. Blood sport. Touching my wound, I was reminded of Samuel Johnson's description of angling as, "a stick, a string, with a fish at one end and a fool at the other." In my case, he was half right.

I worked my way upstream, wading in water past my ankles. On the left bank, a dragonfly hovered and glided over a patch of equisetum. Ancient insect, ancient plant. A scene that has gone on for some 200 million years. Same-old same old.

I heard a *clack-ack-ack* and looked up to see a belted kingfisher wing its way upstream. The bird perched on a branch directly across the stream. The kingfisher had better luck than I, clutching in its beak a fingerling trout. The little fish arched and flexed mightily. The bird was not about to let go, but couldn't manage to swallow this squirming thing either. It looked as if the wiggling fingerling might escape the bird's death grip when, so quickly I thought I might have imagined it, the bird flicked its crested head. *Wham!* It slammed the fish against the branch.

The fish went still for a moment, then resumed its wiggling. *Wham!* The bird slammed the fingerling again. The bird pointed the stunned fish down its throat and swallowed it in a gulp. The bird cocked its head as if to say: "Catch-and-release, my ass." And flew off.

There, I thought, was a bird Pvt. Silas Goodrich would have loved.

HISTORY OFFERS ONLY THE FAINTEST SKETCH of Pvt. Silas Goodrich. Silas hailed from Massachusetts. He was one of the youngest members of the Lewis and Clark Expedition, although we don't know his exact birth date. He was a soldier in the new American army in January 1804 when he was transferred to the command of Capt. Meriwether Lewis. In order to make the expedition, we know he was a hale and hearty type at the start.

Mostly, we know that Private Goodrich loved to fish. Like St. John of the New Testament, Silas fished his way into history. Silas was probably a bait fisherman of humble, worm-drowning stock. When the expedition wanted fish, they wasted little worry over sport. Near the Continental Divide, the expedition built a seine out of dogwood and willow stems and netted some 528 trout and a dozen grayling. In the headwaters of the Salmon River in Idaho, salmon were spawning in the tributaries and expedition members shot them with their Kentucky long rifles.

But Silas's fishing wasn't all work. We know that the Corps of Discovery left St. Louis with a stash of twenty-eight hundred steel fishhooks, which they used primarily as trade goods with the native tribes. In the wilderness, five small hooks were worth two beaver pelts. But not all the hooks were traded. Silas made good use of the rest.

My mental picture of Silas Goodrich is as much imagination as historical record. I picture Silas walking along a riverbank—the Missouri or the Jefferson or the Clearwater—cutting a willow stem with a pocketknife. He ties on the slimmest string to the stick and ties a hook to the string. He kicks open a buffalo chip or a rotten cottonwood log and grubs up a grub. From there, he proceeds to land some of the finest catches you could ever wish for.

Sam Johnson was wrong: Silas Goodrich was no fool. Silas could catch anything. Often, Silas's catch of the day was a new biological discovery. Early in the expedition, along where the Missouri River now makes the border between Nebraska and Iowa, Silas landed an enormous channel catfish, the first on scientific record. Days later he and another expedition member landed a mess of blue catfish that weighed an average thirty pounds apiece. Farther upstream on the Missouri, he became the first white man on written record to land a sauger. His line also collected the first specimen of the goldeye. But his most famous success came the evening of June 13, 1805.

Here's the story: The expedition was in crisis. The Corps was heading up the Missouri River, towing their loaded boats against the spring flow. They had been at this for fifty-six days, ever since leaving their winter camp among the Mandans in North Dakota in early April.

The Mandans had given the captains directions to the headwaters of the Missouri. They foretold the pertinent landmarks, such as the mouths of the Yellowstone, Musselshell, and Milk Rivers. But in June the expedition came upon a distressing puzzle. The Missouri River branched. The two forks looked largely identical. If the Indians had said something about this big fork in the river, the explorers lost it in the interpretation. The instructions from Thomas Jefferson were explicit: Follow the Missouri to its source. The Indians had told the Corps to look for a mighty waterfall. The waterfall was on the Missouri. But no one said anything about a fork.

"An interesting question was now to be determined," wrote

Lewis. "Which of these rivers was the Missouri? . . . Thus our cogitating faculties have been busily employed all day."

The men paced the banks, examining the evidence. The rivers were of roughly equal size. One river was rocky and clear, the other muddy and with a clay bottom. Did the cloudy river pick up its sediment on a long trip across the plain? Did the clear, rocky stream tumble more directly out of the mountains? Lewis led a party up the northern fork, but found nothing to settle the question.

The expedition studied, fretted, argued. In the end, the opinion of the expedition was split according to rank. The enlisted men, including Silas Goodrich, thought the Corps should take the muddy northern fork. The two captains figured the correct stream was the clear, southern branch. The success or failure of the entire expedition rested on this one question and everyone knew it. But there was only one way to find out for certain. Go look for the big falls.

The captains, in the end, made the call. The Corps would move up the southern fork. Lewis would take a few men and forge ahead. Clark and the larger party would pull their gear upstream. Lewis took his men, Silas Goodrich among them, and sallied forth.

Lewis's patrol climbed out of the Missouri River canyon and walked across the cactus plain. They marched upstream, noting vast herds of bison and shooting a couple grizzly bears. Toward the end of the day, the men noted an enormous plume of white smoke rising from the prairie. Only they came to realize it was not smoke. It was mist. This was the Great Falls of the Missouri. The riddle was solved.

The scene was overwhelming: The entire volume of the mighty Missouri spilling over not one, but over five towering cascades. The water tumbled and frothed and roared over a stairway of bedrock, falls ranging from fifteen to fifty feet high, stretching over miles of river. Even the river between the falls was an angry froth of whitewater. It was one of the two largest waterfalls ever seen by European man, only slightly smaller than Niagara. Lewis was both elated and chagrined. On one hand, he had determined which fork was the Missouri. But on the other, he was beginning to realize how monumental a task it would be to portage the expedition's equipment around this obstacle. Aside from the Bitterroot Mountains of Idaho, the Great Falls constituted the most formidable obstacle the expedition would face. It would take twenty-five grueling days to portage their gear the twenty-five miles around the waterfalls.

Faced with this spectacle, Pvt. Silas Goodrich went fishing. It was June, and the weather was mild. It had rained recently, so we know the air was clear, the distant horizon sharp. The evening stretched long toward the summer solstice. The sap was rising in the willow stem Silas cut for a pole and the wild rose was in full, fragrant bloom. The yellow warblers and western kingbirds sang a musical riot in the riverside tree canopy, as they still do. The sound of the water was deafening and the mist beaded on Silas's beard and eyelashes. Silas walked to the foot of these tremendous falls and flicked his baited hook into the depths.

The trout were big, firm, and silver, a full eighteen inches long and weighing a couple pounds apiece. They took the hook gently, but then fought hard, not breaking the surface explosively like a rainbow trout but holding firm in the river depths like a cutthroat will. I can imagine how these fish fought, how Silas pulled in the line, hand over hand. It had been months, perhaps years, since Silas had caught a trout back in Massachusetts, but the shape and tug of this fish must have reminded him instantly of the brook trout he knew back home. I imagine that Silas let out a yelp of delight upon seeing the fish, their chromium sheen and cheetah spots.

It is easy for me to imagine this evening as one of the richest, most beautiful in Silas's brief life. In the glow of the long evening, he returned to camp with six fine trout. These fish were not just dinner. They were the first cutthroat trout introduced to science, lightly breaded and seasoned with salt and pepper. Quite subjectively, Lewis described the trout as "sumptuous."

Before noting the quality of his meal, Lewis described the trout in detail. In particular he noted the black speckling on the fish's flanks and the bright red slashes under its chin, as if the fish were displaying a cowboy's silk scarf or perhaps a slash of blood. Decades later the sporting press coined a common name for the fish based on these same markings: the Montana blackspot. A later name stuck: the cutthroat.

Since Lewis's initial description, ichthyologists have divided the cutthroat trout into fourteen subspecies, under the species *Oncorhynchus clarki*. Goodrich's catch was the archetypal subspecies *Oncorhynchus clarki lewisi*. The Lewis and Clark trout. Goodrich's name was forgotten by taxonomists, even though he clearly caught the fish and, most likely, cleaned and filleted them as well.

The fish we call trout developed 50 million years ago, after the great extinction that killed the dinosaurs. Some 15 million years ago, a proto-trout split the lineage into two stems, the fall-spawning char, such as Dolly Varden and brook trout, and the spring-spawning true trout, including the rainbow and cutthroat. Gradually the world spun into the Pleistocene, a couple million chilly years that plunged North America into and out of the grip of glaciers. Ice sheets scoured the Northern Hemisphere. Giant freshwater lakes welled behind enormous dams of earth and ice, breaking out in apocalyptic floods and then forming again. Advancing sheets of ice carved streambeds into waterfalls, while they shunted tributaries from one river drainage to another and rivers from one ocean to another.

The streams flowing directly into the ocean were exploited by sea-run trout, which worked their way upstream. The chaotic world of water and ice divided and isolated trout populations. These isolated populations took on their own characteristics, adapting to thrive under local conditions and eventually becoming species and further dividing into subspecies.

This is the world in which the cutthroat was born. Isolated drainages spawned individual subspecies. There is the Yellowstone cutthroat of Yellowstone Lake and its rivers. The Snake River fine-spot cutthroat exists in the Snake River drainage. The rivers of the Southwest host the fish known as the greenback and the Gila cutthroat. The upper Columbia Basin, including Washington, Idaho, and Montana, right down to Griffin Creek, hosts the westslope cutthroat.

You may note that Silas Goodrich landed his specimens of westslope cutthroat on the *east* side of the Continental Divide, in the Missouri drainage. Fish biologists believe that in the recent geological past, westslope cutthroat trout hurdled the Continental Divide at Summit Lake, now encompassed in southern Glacier National Park. Summit Lake is a pretty pond that is remarkable in that it has outlets at both ends, one flowing into the Atlantic watershed and one into the Pacific. From here, westslope cutthroat colonized the upper basins of the Missouri. Summit Lake is in a striking location, perched near timberline with sweeping alpine vistas on all sides and a high ridge of ancient limestone directly to the north. The most noteworthy geological feature here is a jagged folding of rock called the Lewis Overthrust. The nearby highway crosses what is called Marias Pass, indirectly named for Meriwether Lewis's heartthrob, Maria Wood.

Cutthroat trout are widely known as easy fish to catch. Anglers sometimes deride them as gullible, since they will strike at almost anything, including at times a bare hook. I have tossed twigs into wilderness streams and watched trout bite them and shake them before spitting them out. In Yellowstone Park, researchers found that a native cutthroat trout is caught and released on average eight times a year. Meanwhile, an imported German brown trout in the same water is caught and released only once.

But this habit is not properly described as naivete. A bass that grows fat and old in some warm, productive bayou of Louisiana can afford to be choosy about what it eats. A trout that survives in clear, almost distilled water at the outlet of a glacier cannot. It strikes at what comes its way.

To this day, westslope cutthroat trout demand the kind of waters in which they evolved. The water must be cold. It must be clean. It must have an ample supply of aquatic and semiaquatic insects. The stream must have beds of gravel—fine, but not too fine—where the fish can spawn and where the eggs can survive. The trout evolved in waters generally without other species of trout and fare poorly among competition.

These prerequisites have left the fish vulnerable to the ways of modern humans.

The cutthroat trout has been lost from stream after stream, lake after lake. One subspecies is already extinct and several others, including the westslope, are in trouble. Anglers and biologists noticed declines in westslope cutthroat in the 1940s and '50s. The westslope was on the federal "red book" of troubled species in 1966. But when the Endangered Species Act passed in 1973, taxonomical arguments kept the fish off the protected list. Now, many years later, it is still a candidate for protection under the Endangered Species Act.

Livestock, particularly cattle, trample riverbanks and make cutthroat streams muddy and warm. Spawning beds are easily smothered by dust and silt from ore trucks, log skidders, and bulldozers. Mine waste can poison streams, while irrigation pumps draw down rivers, leaving streams unnaturally shallow and warm.

Fishing has mixed effects on the cutthroat. On one hand, anglers are traditionally the champions of their prey and have helped conserve fish around the world. A dedicated brand of anglers, such as the members of Trout Unlimited, have fought as hard as anyone to protect native fish. However, anglers have also been part of the problem for cutthroat trout. Humans can catch cutthroat trout faster than the fish can reproduce, making them vulnerable to overfishing.

Some anglers grow bored with the ease of fishing for cutthroat—as if the purpose of the fish is simply to provide a few moments of entertainment. The anglers—and the agencies funded with fishing license dollars—have a sad history of introducing brook, rainbow, and brown trout to cutthroat streams. The exotics tend to hybridize with cutthroats or introduce disease and unnatural competition. Often the cutthroats are eliminated altogether.

Westslope cutthroat trout are gone from about 90 percent of

streams that historically supported them. Pyramid Lake, Nevada, which offered forty-pound cutthroat in the 1920s, was diverted for irrigation and its cutthroat fishery was largely destroyed. The Great Falls of the Missouri have been almost completely dammed for hydropower generation. If Silas Goodrich were to return to the tailwater of the Great Falls, he could cast until his rotator cuff wore out and never land another cutthroat.

THAT WAS NOT QUITE THE STATE OF AFFAIRS I encountered at Griffin Creek. There was no anglers' trail beaten along the banks. No empty beer cans or wasted wads of monofilament. The tracks of moose and mink were the only ones I found on shore. Though the stream flows almost entirely though public, national forest land, it is still beleaguered by the plagues of the trout world.

Exotic trout—namely brook trout—have infested Griffin Creek. Brookies are native back East, but often disastrous to the native life of Western streams. Only the waterfall I visited earlier keeps the invaders at bay. Cattle graze the upstream meadows, damaging the stream there. The local chapter of Trout Unlimited has erected barbed wire fences to keep the cows out, but the stream will take decades to heal, if it can at all. The forest around Griffin Creek has been scalped in big, square clear-cuts. Loggers left a buffer strip of standing trees along the creek, but the spring snowmelt no longer follows natural patterns, and the logging roads send silt to the streams. The watershed has been altered for a generation to come. I asked the local Forest Service biologist about Griffin Creek. "The watershed is just unraveling," she said. "It's a miracle the fish are there at all."

But the trout *are* still here. At least for now. Little, but strong and silver and perfectly proportioned. They dimple the surface with their feeding. Heroic fish. Survivors.

I tried to read the water like a trout, like a kingfisher or a mink. The stream was crosshatched with downed logs, which offer cover from my hook and from osprey talons. The water tumbled over shallows, mixing oxygen in the water. The oxygen gives life to insects, which give life to fish, which offer both spiritual and physical nutrition to me. I have no qualms about my place in this food chain. And I have no qualms about the fact that I enjoy this little hunt, even if the fish most certainly does not. I imagine the kingfisher and the mink enjoy their work as well. Certainly there is no sin in that. The sin comes with the greed and the pride, not the pursuit itself. The hook hurts the fish, I cannot dispute that, but probably no more than the talons of an osprey or the teeth of an otter.

As an angler who favors cutthroat trout, I do release fish. We must, or there will shortly be no cutthroat left. But I am not strictly a catch-and-release fisherman. To justify in my mind this rough treatment of beautiful fish, I must take a few home for the pan. If a stream is so heavily fished that it cannot spare even a single fish, then I figure that water needs a rest altogether. This logic may make sense to no one but myself, but little of fishing makes sense to anyone but the fisher.

I knelt on the grassy bank, like a supplicant to the river. I tried to keep my profile, my shadow, off the water. I cocked my little rod and flipped the lure into the flow. The lure bounced off a downed log, then dropped into a deep spot in the stream.

Westslope cutthroat trout are almost entirely insectivores. They generally do not eat other fish. Although it's impossible to say what goes on in the mind of a trout, it probably takes on the lure as a trespassing fish. That's the reason the cutthroat wear those famous red throat patches: The cutthroat flashes them at rival fish when driving them out of its territory.

My little cast was perfect. I flicked a little tension into the line and reeled in the lure. I felt voltage in the strike. I snapped my wrist—quick, but not too quick. The fish was on, fighting for its life. I raised the tip of my rod and giggled a little. I turned the reel handle a couple times. I felt the will of the fish resisting my will. Then, the line went slack.

Missed. Rats. Silas, I thought, I could use some advice here.

FISHING, we know, was not the only carnal delight in which Silas Goodrich partook. In the dreary, rainy winter at Fort Clatsop when the Corps ate moldy elk meat and fought a constant infestation of fleas, Silas took an interest in at least one native woman. The result of this coupling was not a happy one.

"Goodrich has recovered from [syphilis] which he contracted from an amorous contact with a Clatsop damsel," Lewis wrote. "I cured him . . . by the uce of murcury."

There is an ongoing debate as to whether Europeans introduced syphilis to North Americans, or whether it was the other way around. Some authorities believe that men under the command of Christopher Columbus took the disease home to Europe after contracting it in the West Indies. Others maintain the disease, like smallpox and alcoholism, was among the miseries introduced upon the people of the New World. The Clatsops, it is clear, suffered badly from syphilis. Lewis gave Silas the usual treatment of the day: pills that were pretty much straight mercury.

Nowadays, antibiotics are a cure for syphilis, but Lewis's dollop of mercury was not. In fact, the metallic liquid is deadly poisonous, eventually causing permanent and lethal damage to the brain, liver, and kidneys.

After the mercury treatment, Goodrich's symptoms faded. Lewis was satisfied with the effectiveness of this treatment, but he was mistaken. We now know that such apparent remission is a standard course for syphilis and in no way indicates a cure. The disease may remain dormant for years before recurring. When it does, the results are dreadful: the disease manifests itself in destruction of internal organs, paralysis, psychosis and, eventually, death.

On the home stretch of the expedition, in July 1806, the "pox" had returned to Silas Goodrich and he suffered badly. He made it home safely and was healthy enough to reenlist with the army. But it is not surprising that Silas did not survive long after his return from the West at the end of his tour of duty. He died before he was forty. We don't know the cause of his death— whether disease, metal poisoning, or perhaps something else entirely. But Silas's ill fortune has been of renewed interest to historians for a completely nonmedical reason.

For all that we know about the Lewis and Clark Expedition, actual physical evidence of the journey is almost nonexistent. Historians are able to roughly trace the trail through the explorers' notes and descriptions. But historians find these maddeningly vague. They wish to pinpoint locations—for example, the exact place where Fort Clatsop sheltered the Corps through the winter of 1805–06. About the only physical evidence of their presence is Clark's signature carved into a natural pillar of stone near Billings, Montana. The crew's boats, their clothes, and their shelters, were all organic and have rotted into oblivion. Historians are eager to pin down the exact trail of the Lewis and Clark Expedition. Silas's disease may help them do that.

Mercury is an element. The body cannot metabolize it. Nor does mercury decay or otherwise break down once outside the human body. The body recognizes it as poison and expels as much of the heavy metal as possible through urine. So in theory, wherever Silas Goodrich urinated should still show traces of mercury. Historians are sifting through the forest mulch of Fort Clatsop and other sites along the Lewis and Clark Trail, looking for clues that indicate latrine sites. In any they find, they will then look for traces of mercury to help confirm that the expedition did, indeed, pass that way.

TIME. "Time is but a stream I go a-fishin' in." Thoreau said that. On this stream, time took its leave of me. I looked up to see the shadows stretch hard toward dusk. I had no clear idea how far I had wandered up this stream, but knew I would walk out in the dark. My creel contained my pocketknife, little tackle box, an empty water bottle, and a candy bar wrapper. But no fish. I had caught and released several small trout, but landed none large enough for the pan.

I came to a place in the stream that was wide and slow—not a place where I expected to find a trout. But then, what do I know? I could not see into the water. I didn't notice any trout rising to pluck mosquito larvae off the surface. But it was getting late so I gave it one last try. I flipped the little lure into the water and made my retrieve.

Suddenly, savagely, the line tightened and the rod bowed. I

nearly dropped the rod before my grip tightened. The hooked fish dove under a downed spruce, taking cover. It was a brittle skeleton of a tree, branches sticking out in every direction. I pulled the tip of the rod up, pulling the fish short, to keep it from tangling the line in that mess.

I reeled in the line eagerly. The fish flashed once at the surface and I saw that, for this small water, this was indeed a fine trout. I reeled the fish toward me, then knelt in the mud at the stream bank. I pulled the fish to the shallows, and dunked my right hand to wet it before touching the fish's delicate skin.

The trout was tired. Its gills pumped, the fish equivalent of panting, pulling oxygen from the water to refresh its muscles. The fish was perhaps ten inches long, the largest I have ever seen in Griffin Creek. It was a glistening silver fish, with its black speckling and swashbuckling swath of red on the throat. Gently, my wet hand gripped the fish behind the gills.

I removed the fish from water, its muscle firm under my fingers. The little hook was barely embedded in the corner of the jaw. I pinched the shaft, gave a slight pull, and the hook came out leaving no visible mark. I returned the fish to its liquid world, holding it in a gentle fist. The gills worked, smooth and not the least bit panicked. I thought of the fish rolled in flour and almonds, then fried in olive oil. I recalled Lewis's word: sumptuous.

Then, my fingers opened. The fish floated above my open hand for a second, perhaps not aware that it had been released. Then the spell was broken. The fish flashed silver once and was gone.

Chapter 7

The Last Dancing Prairie

COLUMBIA SHARPTAIL GROUSE
Tympanuchus phasianellus columbianus

SPRING IN MONTANA IS SOMETHING YOU FEEL IN YOUR bones. The season is not so much solar as internal. Even before dawn. Even before coffee.

Karen and I stood on a deserted country road in the dark. South of us, the distant glow of lights marked a Montana mill town called Eureka. This narrow plain spreading darkly on all sides is known as the Tobacco Valley. Kasanka Mountain and its cohorts in the Galton Range loomed to the east, timbered slopes draping down from the horizon like a priest's cloak. The alpine ridges were capped with a full season's snow, although hardy native flowers bloomed on the valley floor. The gibbous moon had set, the sun was not yet up. The last star had just faded.

Louis Young wore a wool cap with a visor, insulated coveralls, and a trim, salt-and-pepper beard. We had arrived in this secret place in Louis's old Ford Bronco. Like everyone in Eureka, Louis works directly or indirectly for the timber industry. He is a biologist for the U.S. Forest Service. His job largely entails assessing the impacts of logging on a portion of the Kootenai National Forest. But this morning he included us in his avocation, not his work. Every word Louis spoke was a soft one, as if he were including us in some benevolent conspiracy.

Louis carried a small knapsack over his shoulders, the legs of a tripod protruding like arrows from a quiver. He found the faint imprint of an elk path, and we followed it into the prairie dawn. Chalky pellets indicated the animals that winter here have scattered back into the foothills, following the receding snowline. We saw our breath as we walked and puffed, but the mildness in the air promised a coming warmth. The soft ground gave slightly underfoot, but wouldn't take a print.

We entered a block of property known as the Dancing Prairie Preserve in far northwestern Montana. The Nature Conservancy, a private outfit that buys and preserves scraps of the world's natural fabric, bought this land to protect a rare type of grassland habitat. Every April for more than a decade, Louis has ventured into this little prairie. He generally comes alone, before sunup and before work. Off to the north, we heard the industrial breathing of a distant sawmill and the occasional hum on the U.S. Highway 93. Only a few house lights twinkled, nearly a mile away. But all this seemed distant. We had come to watch a dance. A dance ancient and primal. A dance that could not be more tenuous.

LOUIS BOWED TO A BARBED WIRE FENCE, then turned and spread the bottom strand with the instep of his boot. Karen handed her camera bag over and followed him into new territory. On my turn I snagged my Levis, tearing denim but not dermis.

Down the fence line, a western meadowlark perched on the top wire. He wore the uniform of his breed—saffron shirt with a black tie—and bellowed his territorial tune. Song staked out the bird's territory on this grassland, as the grid of metal thorns and steel posts staked out our own.

Lewis and Clark were explorers, but were also bird-watchers. These days, the word *bird-watchers* conjures images of codgers in damp sneakers, nattering on about stray housecats and organic sunflower seeds. The captains were of a different stripe: militarists not above observing a new species and then potting it. But they were dedicated and skilled observers, working without the benefit of checklists, Peterson field guides, or recordings of birdsong on compact disc. Historians credit the pair with discovering fifty-one avian varieties, counting subspecies. Two North American passerines are named for the pair: the Lewis's woodpecker, a small woodpecker of a glossy green so deep the bird appears black, and the Clark's nutcracker, a mousy gray corvid with black-and-white wings and tail.

Lewis could not miss the western tanager, a color-burst of a finch with a cayenne-red head and mango-yellow body. The western tanager appears like something out of the jungles of Central America. In fact it is, summering in the Rockies and wintering in the tropics. The expedition also captured alive the cheeky black-billed magpie, a bird so bold it snatched scraps from the crew's plates. The magpie is two feet long, carrying half its length in tail. The magpie is so ubiquitous that Western observers frequently overlook its simple beauty. At first glance, the magpie appears monochromatic black and white, but upon close examination the black becomes iridescent purple and lustrous green, the white a palest blue. In the Pacific surf, Lewis noted the western grebe—a surf-fisher similar to a loon. The western grebe was later split into two species, one dubbed the Clark's grebe. The Clark's grebe, how-ever, is named for another ornithologist, not our explorer.

Both explorers noted new birds, but Lewis was the more expert. An image of Meriwether Lewis emerges from his journals, day after day. He marched twenty miles through broken country. He faced difficult decisions, with unknown but always vital con-sequences. He was deep in uncharted territory. His troops were weary and trail-battered. He was surrounded by unknown and unseen natives who may very well take his presence as hostile. And he ended the day by jotting down a bird list.

The captain's fascination with birds was not simply aesthetic. Recording bird sightings was one of the expressed commands of President Thomas Jefferson, since the return of birds to an unknown territory is an important clue to that land's climate. But clearly, Lewis enjoyed this portion of his mission. What's more, he was good at it. When Lewis added a new bird to his "life list" he was often adding it to the ledgers of science as well. A telling example was the western meadowlark.

As Lewis marched across Montana in the summer of 1805, the song of the western meadowlark caught his ear. Meadowlarks were known as "old field larks" in the grassy pastures of Virginia. The eastern meadowlark looks virtually identical to the western species, but these new birds puzzled him. Their song was an altogether different trill from that which Lewis had heard in the plantations of Virginia. In fact, western and eastern meadowlarks are distinct species, maintaining separate ranges and generally not interbreeding. Even though the birds are indistinguishable visually, they are distinguishable to the ear. Lewis noticed the bird's new song in his journals, and can thus be credited with discovering the western variety.

Lewis took special pains to record economically valuable species—that is, birds that could provide a meal. For example, passenger pigeons were an important human food source in the early 1800s, when 5 billion of them flew over North America. Lewis and Clark noted passenger pigeons clear to the Lemhi Range of Idaho. (Of course, this was not to endure. The last passenger pigeon died in 1914.)

Lewis took particular interest in grouse—meaty, tasty little birds related to chickens. Lewis's eye for detail comes through in his observations. Upon plucking a blue grouse, for instance, Lewis noted the bird had eighteen tail feathers. He knew that was the same number as in the tail of the ruffed grouse common east of the Mississippi. Of the ten members of the grouse family native to North America, four were first scientifically recorded by Meriwether Lewis. In the Rockies he noted the blue and spruce grouse. In the prairies he recorded the bulky sage grouse and the more diminutive sharptail.

Grouse tend to not migrate great distances, instead surviving winter with their bulk and their thick cloaks of down. Their feet are covered in feathered boots that extend to the toes. Certain species grow small scales on their feet every winter, which serve exactly like snowshoes. Other species bury themselves in soft snow, letting blizzards rage overhead as they doze insulated under the white powder. Sharptail grouse, for example, can withstand Alaskan winters without so much as a tree to hide behind.

Sharptail grouse are small for their breed, about eighteen inches long and weighing a couple pounds. They are a dappled brown, with long, pointed tail feathers. Picture a tawny bantam with a punk-rock tail and you're pretty close. In April 1804, when the expedition crossed what is today South Dakota, Lewis first flushed great coveys of sharptail grouse. It was spring, and Lewis noted the birds were dancing. Later the expedition caught a sharptail alive, and kept it in a cage with the idea of shipping it to Jefferson, along with a few live magpies and a prairie dog. The grouse never made it downstream, and I suspect someone entrusted with transporting the fowl may have instead roasted it.

During the Oregon winter of 1805–06, Lewis had long rainy hours to update his journals by candlelight. That winter at Fort Clatsop, Lewis described the sharptail grouse down to its toenails. He also noted seeing the birds on the western side of the Continental Divide. Since then, the American Ornithological Union, the professional society which sorts the taxonomy of birds, has divided the sharptail into several sub-species. Lewis recorded two of those: the Great Plains and Columbian subspecies.

THE DANCING PRAIRIE WAS A LANDSCAPE of native grass, edged with ponderosa pine. The preserve looks like a golf course neglected during a long and bitter groundskeepers strike. The Dancing Prairie's open, rolling terrain is the kind of landscape that has pleased the aesthetic senses of our species since we first roamed the African savanna. The Nature Conservancy prizes it not only for its small population of native grouse, but also for its rich carpet of native grasses, sedges, and forbs. Lewis and Clark walked through similar prairie in interior Washington and north-central Idaho and the valleys of western Montana, although virtually all of that has since been converted to agriculture.

The Dancing Prairie rolled out before us, not so much a sea of grass as a lake of it. A lake one could swim across, if one were hard-pressed. To the east, the preserve was bordered by a road, and then the grassland is converted into the groomed green of irrigated timothy hay. A thin, straight scratch across the preserve showed where some anonymous laborer attempted to irrigate this plot as well, but failed.

Within the bounds of the Dancing Prairie, the earth's surface was tawny as a puma. The land rose and dipped in sensuous waves before giving way to the forested foothills of the Galton Range. Random boulders—the litter tossed out the window by past glaciers—were patterned with orange and green lichen. The low spots, where moisture collects, was thick with new ryegrass sprouting through a thatch of previous generations. But most of the soil was thin, scattered bunchgrass and fescue growing amid the tiny upheavals of molehills. The grass was ankle high—perfect for delivering its annoying, itchy seed heads into our socks. In other, more moist regions of the Pacific Northwest, similar grasslands now grow one hundred bushels of wheat per acre. With meager soil and precipitation, however, the Dancing Prairie is too dry to cultivate or even graze hard. So we wrap a fence around it and call it natural.

Which, so far, has been the salvation of these grouse. The Dancing Prairie Preserve, Louis Young tells us, is one of the last places the Columbia sharptail grouse dwells in Montana.

American history has been hard on prairie grouse. Specifics vary with location, but our tendency to plow and graze every plot of fertile ground has left very little space for prairie grouse. The heath hen is gone altogether, the last one seen on Martha's Vineyard in Massachusetts in 1931. Both the greater and lesser prairie chicken of the country's midriff are also much diminished. Even the sage grouse, which lives on the largely unwanted high desert of the American West and is not particularly good to eat, is a candidate for threatened status.

Prairie grouse represent a classic example of the effects of island biogeography. That is, the larger an "island" of habitat, the more stable the populations of flora and fauna. The patches of prairie have been diced smaller and smaller, as cultivation, highways, and cities close in from every side. As the islands of habitat grow smaller, they fail to support grouse over the long run. Homebody birds like grouse are especially prone to local extinctions, since they rarely receive fresh blood from distant gene pools.

Lewis's two subspecies of sharptail grouse—the Plains and the Columbia—have fared quite differently over the past two hundred years. On the arid Great Plains, where the land is often too dry for cultivation, the Plains sharptail grouse thrives. Shotgunners in North Dakota, for example, kill one hundred thousand of the subspecies annually without harming the overall population. Ironically, industrialization sparked the spread of Plains sharptail grouse in the upper Midwest. When northern spruce and white pine forests were logged and burned in Michigan, Wisconsin, and Minnesota, the ground was converted from forest to prairie. Plains sharptail grouse spread north.

Conversely, the Columbia sharptail grouse subspecies has literally been plowed under. A few strong populations exist in Idaho and Washington, British Columbia, and elsewhere. But Columbia sharptails are gone from Oregon. In Montana, only small, very vulnerable populations remain, including the dancing birds of this dancing prairie.

TO UNDERSTAND PRAIRIE GROUSE, Louis Young said, one must understand the lek. This was where he leads us. To this lek.

Humans stake property lines with fences. Coyotes with snow stained yellow. Songbirds—like the meadowlark—define their territories and woo their mates with their voices. But prairie grouse like sharptails exploit another strategy altogether. Sharptails are drab, quiet birds. If the males were to scatter themselves all across the prairie, as larks do, females would have a slim chance of finding them. So instead of singing, the male grouse gather each spring in dancing circles called leks, held in the same locations. Lek comes from the Swedish term, *leka*—to play. To human eyes, these secret playgrounds look like every other acre nearby. But the lek is vital to the sharptail's survival.

Grouse dance in the spring, the instinct triggered by the gradual lengthening of days. The spring tells them it's time to get serious.

The males gather at the lek and dance in circles. The birds strut and puff and burble. They posture and preen. They jockey for position. The older, more prime males dance in the middle of the concentric circles. Young birds, the less desirable males, the reproductive riffraff, are kept to the outer rings.

The females arrive, one by one, to admire the males. It's a meat market, and the females do the shopping. The female selects the male with the liveliest step, the one that has earned choice position within the circle. The two join for a brief fling. Tryst over, the hen goes away, scratches a shallow nest on the prairie floor and (if she avoids the skunks, ravens, weasels, and house-cats) raises her brood alone. After mating, the male resumes his place in the dancing circle, waiting for another opportunity to father a brood.

Barring some new discovery, Louis explains, the Dancing Prairie Preserve contains the last Columbia sharptail lek in Montana. The grouse meet to dance every spring at the same nondescript patch of grassland. The institutional memory is lodged in their pea-brains. If a local grouse population dies out—say from disease or an off-season blizzard—the memory of the lek dies with it. Individual grouse may recolonize the prairie, but without the lek they will probably not breed successfully.

The lek is vital to the survival of the prairie grouse, but is also their Achilles' heel. Here, grouse are at their most vulnerable. During the market hunting era of the 1800s, hundreds of thousands of prairie grouse of all species were slaughtered in killing binges as gunners concentrated their efforts at the leks. This lek has been protected from hunting for years, but continues to dwindle to a mere handful of birds. The dangers now come from rural subdivisions, which chop up the land and send dogs and cats through the preserve. Louis knows full well he may come here one spring and find no birds at all.

"The birds are hanging on," Louis said. "That's about the most that can be said for them. They're hanging on by their toenails."

Desperate times call for desperate measures. In past years, Louis and biologists from the Montana Department of Fish, Wildlife and Parks have traveled to British Columbia to collect reinforcement birds. They netted the birds at a Canadian lek, holding the birds in old liquor boxes. The cardboard bottle separators prevented the birds from pecking at each other. They loaded the crates in the back of a pickup truck and shuttled them south of the border, like Prohibition bootleggers hustling crates of whiskey. They released the Canadian birds here. That effort— and blind luck—is why this lek remains active.

Walking across the prairie, Louis stopped at a small rise. He cocked his head. Amid the lark song we heard a strange series of clucks, purrs, and hoots. Now, there was reason to whisper.

"Hear 'em?" he said. And for the first time this morning, I saw the full breadth of Louis Young's smile.

THE KOOTENAI INDIANS lived in the Tobacco Valley before an 1855 treaty confined them to their present reservation north of Missoula. The Kootenai were (and, to some extent, still are) hunter-gatherers. Sharptails were on the menu.

To snare sharptail grouse, Kootenai boys would weave ropes of grass and, later, horsehair. The boys would belly down on the prairie grass and lay out their snares at the grouse leks. When the grouse danced into a waiting loop, the boy would give a yank and catch supper.

Like many native prairie cultures, the Kootenai have a ceremonial dance that mimics the dance of the sharptail grouse. Like the natural dance it is patterned after, the Kootenai grouse dance is performed by males.

The Kootenai were dislodged from the plains of northwestern Montana by the usual combination of law, economics, and force. They were sent to the Flathead Indian Reservation in the Mission Valley, just north of Missoula. Luckier than most tribes, theirs is one of the most beautiful and bountiful reservations in the United States. For the initial decades of the reservation's existence, the Kootenai and their Salish-speaking neighbors maintained communal patches of prairie for the traditional gathering of bitterroot and other plants. Columbia sharptail grouse continued to flourish.

But Anglo farmers eyed that unplowed land with avarice. In 1910, Congress brushed aside past promises and opened the Flathead Indian Reservation to homesteading. Territorial boundaries were lifted. The communal (or as Congress saw it, the underutilized) patches of prairie were handed over for the white man's plow and irrigation ditches.

With intensified cultivation, the sharptails on the reservation dwindled quickly. The Kootenai themselves may have shot them out during the starvation years of the Great Depression. By the 1950s, the birds were scarce on the reservation. The last one was seen in the early 1980s. Another fragment of the Kootenai culture was purloined. A process begun in the days of Thomas Jefferson had culminated in the days of Ronald Reagan.

The first time I wrote about the sharptail grouse of the Dancing Prairie, I received a phone call from a young woman who was a member of the Confederated Salish-Kootenai Tribes. She was a dancer. She was breaking tradition, she told me, by learning a man's dance, the dance of the grouse. But she was afraid that her culture could lose the dance, just as it had lost its grouse. She said she wanted to see the birds dance, as her forefathers had. I gave her Louis's name and telephone number. It is a long drive between the Dancing Prairie and the Flathead Indian Reservation, and the two were unable to arrange a meeting. The best Louis could do was send a videotape.

WHEN THE SUN FINALLY SHOWED ITSELF over the eastern crest, Louis, Karen, and I crouched low and stalked to the top of the next rise. We crawled on all fours. Louis dropped to his belly and we followed suit. Karen unrolled a wool blanket from Louis's knapsack. Louis erected his tripod and fixed a telescope to the mount. He adjusted the focus ring and rolled aside.

"Take a look," he said. We viewed a scene from the century before. Through the telescope, the birds strutted and pranced. They faced off, beak to beak, spreading their wings and fanning their tails. The tails pointed skyward, sharp as arrowheads and white as bleached kerchiefs. The birds stomped their downy feet and inflated purple air sacs on their throats. Yellow eyebrows bristled on their foreheads. Someone once compared their herky-jerk motions and sudden changes in direction to the actions of a windup toy. It's an apt simile.

Occasionally and without warning, the birds flutter-hopped. That is, they launched into the air four feet or so, as if someone had lit a firecracker under their tails. Columbia sharptails evolved in a prairie world without bison, unlike their Great Plains cousins.

And they flutter-hop higher than members of other subspecies. The theory is the Columbia Basin birds had to hop higher to be seen over the ungrazed grass. I wondered, then, if a Kootenai dancer might also jump higher in his dance than a Lakota or Blackfeet dancer on the Great Plains.

Louis squinted through the scope and counted. "Eight," he said. "All males." A northern harrier—a marsh hawk—coasted overhead. The small raptor was an unlikely predator of sharptails, but the grouse took no chances. They flushed, bursting in all directions. Their cupped wings beat loudly, then locked as the birds coasted low into the prairie. We stayed put, and after a quarter-hour the grouse buzzed back like a squadron of fighter jets returning to an air base. We counted incoming birds but again got no higher than eight.

The sky paled. A long-billed curlew (another bird credited to Meriwether Lewis) squealed overhead. Louis noted a merlin falcon perched on a fence post. The morning warmed and began to lose its freshness. Dawn soothed grouse passions. One by one the grouse faded into the grassland, like college kids dispersing after the dance hall closes. No females that morning. We stood from the grass, rolled up the blanket, and folded the tripod. It was time for Louis to get to work. We walked back down the elk path to the road.

Louis's 1968 Ford Bronco awaited us. For the first time, I noticed that the blocky little truck was bright blue. It fairly glowed in the sun, even though the truck was almost as old as me. "Did you repaint it yourself?" I asked.

"No," Louis said. "That's the original paint job." I was surprised by the luster, but perhaps I should not have been. This seems to be Louis's credo: Take care of things. Make them last.

Chapter 8

Bitterroot Ghost Forests

WHITEBARK PINE
Pinus albicaulis

CLARK'S NUTCRACKER
Nucifraga columbiana

ON THEIR EIGHT-THOUSAND-MILE MARCH, MEMBERS OF the Lewis and Clark Expedition fled wounded and enraged grizzly bears. Wind whipped their campfires into prairie conflagrations. They swamped boats midriver, not knowing how to swim. They slipped on cliffs of crumbling sandstone. York was almost washed away in a flash flood. Lewis dodged a bullet shot by a Blackfeet horse thief, and was later shot in the ass in a hunting accident. Another explorer stabbed himself in the thigh with a butcher knife. Bison stampeded through their camp. Half-wild horses threw them onto rocks. One fellow was bitten by a rattlesnake, another by a beaver, another by a wolf.

But this country—the Bitterroot Mountains—nearly ate Lewis and Clark alive. The Lolo Trail crossing was a case-study in misery. Horses fell and smashed their loads, rolling and screaming until slamming to a halt against a downhill tree. Game was scarce. When food was within range, guns misfired. Their native guide got lost.

Here they were deepest in trouble. Here they were deepest in the wilderness. Karen and I arrived to see how much wilderness remained. And the Bitterroot Mountains would gnaw on us pretty good, too.

WHEN WE LEFT THE LOW COUNTRY, the land smoldered and the horizon was a salmon-colored smudge. Sunsets erupted lurid and red through the haze of airborne carbon. Forest fire season was underway. We drove past encampments of Forest Service infantry, men and women uniformed in vivid yellow shirts, green jeans, and combat boots. Helicopters hovered over rivers, dipping enormous buckets into the water to drench the brittle, burning forest.

But all that changed as we drove up Lolo Creek, out of Montana's Bitterroot Valley. Here the forest was lush, dense, and well-watered. Meadows were verdant. Clouds shrouded the ridges. The spruce and hemlock looked as if they had just stepped out of the shower. Nowadays the Lolo Trail is traced roughly by U.S. Highway 12, writhing like a sidewinder and patched like a Juarez inner tube. We stopped at Lolo Hot Springs. A campground, a motel, and a steaming swimming pool have sprouted since the Corps of Discovery soaked here. We wanted to ward off the mountain chill with a thermal swim, but were driven off by amplifiers in the back of a Chevy Blazer, blasting distorted Credence Clearwater Revival.

Karen drove into the clouds as raindrops speckled the cracked windshield. We crossed into Idaho at Lolo Pass, just north of where the Corps crossed. I punched the scan button on the car radio to fetch a weather report. The digital numbers spun through the frequencies. Here, the mountains block out everything.

The Bitterroot Mountains, and neighboring Bitterroot River, are named for a flowering plant, the bitterroot or rock rose. The plant is a traditional staple of the Salish and Kootenai diet, although both Lewis and Clark found its flavor too strong. The plant's scientific name, *Lewisia rediviva*, tells us that Meriwether Lewis is not only credited with discovering this species, but this genus as well.

The bitterroot is a humble, pretty flower, its rose bloom coming in early summer. The plant exists almost entirely underground, its blossom spreading atop the earth's surface. The bitterroot is remarkable for how long it can remain dormant in arid times. Lewis took samples, then pressed and dried them. A sample given to the American Philosophical Society in Philadelphia remained in a dark cabinet for years until a curator checked it. To his surprise the plant had sprouted. He potted the plant and it grew. Which explains the second half of its Latin name: *redi-viva.* The reborn.

"Let's try a book on tape," Karen said. Selections littered the dashboard, most overdue from our county library. I slipped a cassette in the player. The reader's voice spoke, clear and resonant:

We were young and we thought we were tough and we knew it was beautiful and we were a little bit crazy but we hadn't noticed it yet.

The words of Norman Maclean. King of the opening line.

I was surrounded by an ocean of mountains, the voice said. *More mountains than I had ever seen or would ever see again.*

This was from a story in Maclean's book *A River Runs Through It and Other Stories.* The book and subsequent movie turned fly-fishing into a hip fad and helped launch Brad Pitt to movie stardom. But tucked inside that volume is a story of the Bitterroot Mountains—a story as beautiful, neglected, and forgotten as these mountains themselves. We listened as dusk fell into place. Karen and I camped in a quiet stand of lodgepole pine, picturing ourselves young and tough and a little bit crazy on the edge of that beautiful ocean of mountains.

LEWIS AND CLARK left the East knowing Western mountains awaited them. But none of them had seen mountains more rugged than the Appalachians. They figured the Rockies would be roughly similar. The captains hoped for a short portage, then a quick, easy float down the headwaters of the Columbia.

They were wrong. When they arrived at Three Forks, ten-thousand-foot peaks surrounded the source of the Missouri. In early September, after finding the Shoshone Indians of the Lemhi

Mountains, Lewis finally crossed the Continental Divide. The mountains were colder and more rugged than anything he had imagined. Instead of a quick portage, he found a geologic uprising today called the Idaho Batholith—not a *range* of mountains but an enormous *mass* of them. Jagged granite carved by past glaciers, dense with pine, fir, spruce, and cedar. Steep canyons dropped thousands of feet into a ribbon of angry white water the Indians called the River of No Return.

Sacagawea helped Lewis and Clark barter for horses. A Shoshone they nicknamed Toby agreed to guide them north, down the Bitterroot River, up Lolo Creek, then across the Lolo Trail. The men were daunted by these formidable mountains, but remained optimistic. If the Indians could survive in this inhospitable terrain, wrote Lewis, they would as well.

Norman Maclean wasn't the first writer to compare the land to an ocean. From the Sahara Desert to the Kansas wheatlands, the ocean is a handy metaphor for vastness, to describe something that stretches to the horizon and diminishes the human being to insignificance. The Bitterroot Mountains are no sleepy ocean, but instead a storm-whipped North Sea. An ocean full of white-capped tidal waves—tsunamis petrified in granite.

Of the lands that now constitute the fifty United States, the territory that became the state of Idaho was the last to be entered by whites. When Lewis and Clark entered the Bitterroots, the cities of San Francisco, Baltimore, Sitka, and Albuquerque were all well-established. The native people of Idaho—the Lemhi and the Nez Perce—had never seen white men. In many ways, Idaho is the state that has changed the least since the time of the Corps of Discovery. If you want to see a patch of the world as Lewis and Clark saw it, if you want to look out to the horizon and see no sign of industrialized man, if you want to feel your lungs ache and your heart pound as they did, then head for the Bitterroot Mountains.

KAREN AND I DROVE through a tunnel of towering evergreens, their boughs filtering the morning like green prisms. A gravel road led south from Highway 12 and we took it, the wheels pounding the washboard surface. We crossed White Sand Creek. The stream tumbled underneath the bridge, glistening in the sun against the deep shadow of cedar. That was the problem for Lewis and Clark: the dark timber. Clark found the Lolo Trail "Steep & Stoney . . . excessively bad & Thickly strowed with fallen timber."

Under dense trees, no grass grew. No grass meant no bison and only a few elk and mule deer. Usually, the explorers literally ate like wolves. Each man consumed eight pounds of meat per day. The thirty-three members of the Corps happily reduced a bison to bones every day. On the "fat plains of the Missouri," obtaining such provisions was simple. But on the Lolo, the hunters' luck was miserable. The men, Sacagawea, and her little son, Pomp, went hungry.

The Corps ate starvation rations: coyote; crawfish; a couple grouse; old bear grease. They called one stream Colt Killed Creek, because here the captains ordered the men to slay one of their expensive Shoshone colts for supper. The stream is now White Sand Creek. Staring into the dark tunnel of trees, I could imagine the sounds of that hungry night: the whinny of a mare separated from her offspring, the single report of a rifle. The subsequent days grew worse. Their native guide, Toby, lost the trail. Clark forged ahead to find it, but found only more mountains. "From this mountain I could observe high ruged mountains in every direction as far as I could see," Clark wrote. The trail passed "emince Dificuelt Knobs, Stones, much falling timber and emencely Steep." It snowed. "I have been wet and cold as I ever have been in my life," Clark complained, fearing frostbite would cost him his toes.

What a difference a couple centuries make. Karen and I crossed Lewis and Clark's Colt Killed Creek with a week's worth of oatmeal, pasta, dried fruit, and chocolate. We were thrilled by the wilderness around us, not threatened. The road divided the forest like Moses' parting of the Red Sea. We continued south for twenty slow miles, the road climbing and dipping, and did not see another car.

The engine rattled as the road grew steeper. The chassis rattled. We followed the road to the end of the world, to the beginning of everything. The road ended at a Forest Service outpost called Elk Summit, which consisted of a shaggy green meadow, a hoof-beaten corral, and a few picturesque log cabins. We looked for the ranger, but saw no one. Karen rapped on the loose window panes of the patrol cabin. The place was deserted, padlocked tight.

"It's Sunday," I said. "Maybe they're at church."

"It's a long way to church," Karen said. We found a few road-side camps at a small mountain lake. They too were empty.

Eventually we found a squadron of yellow-shirted college kids eating lunch in the back of a green Forest Service pickup. Another fire crew. These firefighters were a mixed bunch. One whiskered fellow had eye sockets dark as ink wells and looked like he never left the wilderness. A striking young woman with ice-blue eyes looked, except for her yellow work shirt and hard hat, like she had stepped straight off a fashion runway in Paris. I unfolded my map on their tailgate and traced our planned route with a finger. The map had not been updated in twenty years, but it was the only one I had. They looked at it thoughtfully, swallowed a mouthful of sandwich, and shrugged. None of them had been there. It wasn't on fire. That's all they knew. We were off.

WE KNEW IT WAS BEAUTIFUL and we were a little bit crazy, but we hadn't noticed it yet.

That opening line from Norman Maclean kept going through my head. It was from a story called *U.S. Forest Service, 1919: The Ranger, the Cook and the Hole in the Sky*. It takes place, in part, at Elk Summit. It is the semiautobiographical story of a young man who fought fires here before helicopters and yellow, fireproof shirts. Maclean wrote it in the 1970s, as an old man remembering his youth. In his day, gear was hauled by mule, and trees were felled with crosscut saws called misery whips. It is the story of a young tough who mouths off to the camp cook at Elk Summit and as punishment is banished into this wilderness. Young Norman was sent to watch for smoke at a mountaintop called Grave Peak, northwest of here.

No one was banishing Karen and me to the wilderness. We were banishing everyone else. We shouldered our packs and set off down a grown-in fire road. The road devolved into a narrow trail. We walked past a faded, unpainted wooden sign, routered letters informing us we were entering the Selway-Bitterroot Wilderness Area. Beyond the sign, all dirt bikes, jeeps, helicopters, even bicycles were officially banned. Here, travel is by foot or by horse.

Everything moves at the same speed it did for Norman Maclean and William Clark and the Nez Perce before them. We stepped down the trail, plodding under the weight of our food, clothing, tent, and sleeping bags. Spruce and larch rose up straight and tall as the masts of old sailing ships. Walls of mountains rose beyond them. Deeper and deeper we went. I found myself thinking of Maclean.

Maclean was raised a preacher's son in Missoula, Montana. He left the West as a young man to pursue a scholarly career at the University of Chicago. Throughout his tenure he summered in Montana and remembered the stories of his youth. He pledged someday to write them down. At age seventy, having retired from his post as literature professor, he completed the task. He left us three slender novellas and a scattering of essays and lectures before dying in 1990 at age eighty-nine. When he started writing, more than fifty summers had passed since Maclean worked with Big Bill Bell and the other legendary firefighting rangers of Elk Summit. Like all great writers, Maclean had an eye for detail and an emphatic demand for accuracy. So he sought out a proofreader to check his facts. He needed someone with a lifetime's experience in these woods. For that, Norman turned to a sage named Bud Moore. As would we. To put Lewis and Clark's discoveries into context with this place, the wilderness.

IN IDAHO, the Corps of Discovery was lost, hungry, and alone. Nonetheless they were still discovering. In the mountains above the Lemhi River, William Clark observed a striking corvid with a mouse-gray body, black wings, and white tail. The bird was the size of a stout crow, but with a chisel of a beak designed to break open pine cones. Clark mistook the bird for a woodpecker, but today it's called Clark's nutcracker.

Days later, as the Corps crested the high country of the Lolo Trail, Meriwether Lewis noted an unusual tree: a pine with five needles to the cluster, like eastern white pine. The branches swept skyward like the antlers of a mule deer. The bark was the color of canvas. This was the whitebark pine.

Lewis and Clark also noticed the forested slopes were black-ened by fire. They figured these burns had been set by Indians trying to clear the route through downed trees. In fact, these fires were probably set by the same force that sets 99 percent of the fires in the Bitterroots today: lightning. The captains were talented naturalists when faced with questions of botany or ornithology. But they were not trained to see the connections of things. No one was.

For that, Karen and I turned to Bud Moore. We met Bud and Janet Moore one January day at their cabin near Condon, Montana. A light snow had fallen the night before and the Moores' yard was speckled with the split-valentine tracks of whitetail deer. Bud greeted us with a tally-ho shout from his woodpile. Bud, then eighty-one, wore a Carhartt jacket that had long ago lost its pigment. He walked us around Coyote Ranch, a woodlot that he works largely alone, from felling the trees with a chain saw, skidding them with a small tractor, and milling them on a portable mill. He showed us the spot where he shot a white-tail buck for winter meat.

"Never did get an elk this year," he said, as another eighty-year-old might comment on a missing Social Security check.

Moore grew up on a homestead along Lolo Creek, not far

from the Lewis and Clark Trail. He was a boy when Maclean was living *A River Runs Through It.* Moore experienced a time when the Lolo Trail was passable to packstock, but not cars. Before he was old enough to shave regularly, he ran an eighty-mile-long trapline. He walked between backcountry cabins alone and on snowshoes, pursuing lynx, pine martens, and other furbearers. One of Moore's trapping cabins was at Wendover Creek, along the Lewis and Clark Trail. The footings of another of his cabins are now under the asphalt of Highway 12.

Karen and I settled into Moore's writing cabin, a small side-building outside the main house. Moore fed scrap lumber into the woodstove, speaking of traplines, Indian wars, and grizzly hunters like a traveler from another time. He never went beyond eighth grade, but it was easy to see why Norman Maclean turned to him for help. Moore grew up with the Forest Service as the outfit metamorphosed from a ragtag band of axmen to a multi-million-dollar federal agency. Better than anyone, Moore knew the Lolo country.

In the 1970s, Maclean came to Moore as a retired Midwestern professor, not a literary icon. His manuscript was roughly typed and wrapped in brown paper. Maclean gave a draft to Moore, asking the forester to check his own knowledge against the recollections in the manuscript. Moore took to the job like he would to felling a big spruce—taking great swings at it. He sat down with the manuscript over his lap and a red pen in his right hand. When he handed the document back to Maclean, the pages looked like Moore might have cut his hand and bled red ink on them.

"I didn't hear from Norman for a month," Moore recalled. "Finally, I ran across him and I asked him about the story. He said: 'God damn it, Bud, *I'm* the college professor, not *you.*'"

Maclean was only partially right. Bud Moore attended graduate studies in the school of the wilderness. Literally, he received an education by fire. Moore's first wage-earning job was fighting a forest fire that burned behind his family's homestead on Lolo Creek. For a backwoods boy in those days, cash was tough to come by. From that fire, Moore's path was clear.

THE FOREST SERVICE has always been a firefighting agency. In the late 1800s, unprecedented forest fires ravaged the upper Midwest. The slash-and-burn timbering of the day left most of Michigan, Minnesota, and Wisconsin as one big tinderbox. Between 1871 and 1894, more than two thousand people burned or suffocated to death in forest fires in those states. Fires scoured the Rocky Mountains whenever lightning and drought conspired. Foremost was the Great Burn of 1910. The Great Burn was fed by an unusual combination of drought and high winds. In a few days, scattered smaller fires erupted into one orange, superheated mass, as if hell had broken into the Bitterroot. Firefighters took after the blaze with shovels, saws, and axes. It proved disastrous. Some two hundred people died in the blaze. When autumn rains finally fell, 3 million acres of Washington, Idaho, and Montana were charred. Vast stands of timber were blackened stalks.

After 1910, the Forest Service became the West's rural fire department. Western politicians won elections by shunting federal dollars into firefighting. Such allocations pleased both the rural landowner, who dreaded the black plumes of smoke, and the timber barons, who appreciated the federal government subsidizing the protection of their assets. Fires had burned this land ever since the glaciers receded, but the government pledged to stop it. Thousands of men (and more than a few women) like Norman Maclean and Bud Moore spent summers perched atop mountains, alone with azimuth instruments and crude telephones. Each summer, lightning storms licked their icy-hot tongues over the mountains. Lookouts kept an eye peeled for smoke. Then they would march after the strike, toting a shovel, ax, and other tools in a packsack. If lightning struck a tree, their job was to fell the tree and snuff the fire. If the fire had spread to the ground, they would trench the blaze.

"The motto was 'Hit 'em hard, keep 'em small,'" Bud Moore said. "If we spotted smoke, we were under standing orders to have it under control by 10 A.M. the next day. It was a discipline that we lived by. There was not a lot of make-believe in that show."

This continued for decades and continues, to some extent, today. Lightning invades in hot afternoons. Lookouts survey the frontier, passing intelligence to headquarters. Commanders bark orders. The infantry hustles in. Smoke jumpers bail out of airplanes like paratroopers behind enemy lines. Thundering sorties of planes dump plumes of pink retardant. A propaganda mill churns out press releases, radio and television messages, even comic books explaining the righteousness of the cause and the totality of the enemy: fire.

The Forest Service was good at its job. They snuffed most of those lightning strikes. Decade by decade, fires became less common. Fewer sparks escaped their strike.

But trees kept growing and kept dying. The dead trees stacked higher and higher. During the dry summers, the woods literally became a storehouse of tinder and kindling. Inevitably, lightning did strike. Some of the fires escaped. Fires became conflagrations that proved impossible to fight and raged unchecked until quashed by fall rains. Big fires were countered with more congressional allocations—bigger budgets for more technology, weaponry, and manpower. Idaho has no glorious wars in its history, no Gettysburg to address or Alamo to remember. Idaho has only the Indian wars and labor strife, which are brutal and disheartening when examined too closely. Instead, Idaho has the war against fire.

Through this smoke and ash emerged Bud Moore, a self-taught expert in the ways of forest fire. Moore was born seven years after the Great Burn. He spent World War II as a marine in the South Pacific, fighting the Japanese. But the rest of his career was with the Forest Service, climbing the ranks of the expanding agency. He become the district ranger near Powell, Idaho, at the ranger station built on the Lolo Trail, along the Lochsa River. As Moore reached middle age, he was plucked out of backwoods Idaho and dropped into the wilderness of Washington, D.C. During the Cold War, he developed strategies for the Defense Department to fight fires that would rage after a nuclear exchange with the Soviets. During this grim assignment, Moore rekindled his spirit by paddling a canoe on the Potomac River, remembering the Bitterroots.

KAREN AND I LEFT Elk Summit on foot, rambling down a well-groomed trail under a blazing summer sun. Our first two days in the Selway-Bitterroot Wilderness were pure delight. The trail was gentle, rambling down rocky ridges and leading us through cirques of alpine lakes and glades of alpine larch. Our escape into the wilderness seemed complete. It seemed like a vigorous vacation. Then, on day three, things went to hell.

Our trail had kept to the high ground. But at this stage of the hike, we had no choice but to plunge off the open ridgelines and into the timbered canyons. We walked out of the high mountain meadows into a dense land of spruce. The trail dropped three thousand feet in elevation and unraveled like a poorly knit sweater. It was as if the land suddenly resented our presence.

The spruce is a shallow-rooted tree that grows in dense groves to stand upright against the rigors of the mountain climate. This works fine for a century or two. But then, when one spruce falls, they all tend to fall at once. One might think that a falling tree would stand a one-in-four chance of falling across a particular trail. Not so. A windstorm had pushed a full 100 percent of the spruces directly between us and where we wanted to go. I counted two hundred deadfalls—that is, blow-down trees—in a single mile of trail. That's one deadfall, on average, every twenty-six feet.

Spruces are full of sharp, brittle limbs that poke at eyes and grab at backpack straps. Karen and I bowed down and crawled under some logs. We did slow-motion hurdles over others, the sandpaper bark scraping our bare legs. We walked around the larger trees altogether.

We carried a week's worth of supplies in our backpacks. Walking wasn't bad, but the bending and crawling were exhausting. Crawling under a log with the weight of a pack was like doing push-ups with a second-grader on your shoulders. Where there was no deadfall, there was brush. Sitka alder. False huckleberry. Mountain ash. The nightmare stuff grew far over our heads and in a dense tangle under our feet. In places, we could see nothing but leaves and stems, not even each other just a few yards apart. We walked hundreds of yards without ever touching the ground, our feet suspended by the springy stems. Walking is an incorrect verb. Bushwhacking is more like swimming. But it is unlike any other form of locomotion. It is more *loco* than *motion.*

When there was no brush and no deadfall, there was bog. Black, knee-deep mud coughed up clouds of fresh-bred mosquitoes. We sweated off insect repellent within moments of applying it. To stop for a gulp of water was to invite a mosquito feast.

We followed a faint erasure of the path. This dissolved in a maze of fragmentary trails. None of the fragments showed any sign of official maintenance. The only things keeping the trails open were moose. Moose, by nature, don't give a damn where they're going or when they'll get there. It's all the same woods to them. They have stilts for legs and are unencumbered by deadfall, bog, or brush. So the moose trails crissed and crossed, deep ruts in some places, faint traces in others, leading us only generally in the direction we wanted to go. The walk was as much a controlled fall as a hike. I heard Karen collapse in a bad spill behind me. She stood up, blood dripping down her shins where rocks had ripped divots from each knee. We bottomed out in the timbered canyon. Shadows grew long and dark, compounded by the depths of the canyon. I had a faint idea that, someday, I was going to have to explain this to a divorce lawyer.

I looked at Karen. Her hair was plastered to her head by sweat. Crushed mosquitoes stuck in bloody splotches on her face. Blood streamed from her wounded knees, mixing with the mud that caked her boots, calves, and shins.

"How are you doing?" I asked.

"How the fuck do you *think* I'm doing?" she asked. Never one to cork up her emotions. We staggered on.

The gradient mellowed somewhat, but the route was still all a-jumble. I felt myself weaken, tripping like a stumblebum over my own boots. Weariness begets clumsiness. Camp, I thought. We need to pitch camp. I refused to consider that we might be lost. The map made perfect sense—except that there was no trail on the ground to match the dashed red line on the paper.

My imagination wandered. What would a twisted ankle or a broken leg mean in this godforsaken hole? If we couldn't walk out, how would anyone find us in this spruce jungle? Who would think to search? No one expected us for a week, and then we had only the foggiest commitments back in civilization. The truck full of firefighters no doubt forgot us as soon as we said good-bye. First things first, I told myself. First, find the damn trail.

As night's shadow began to claim our side of Earth, we broke into a boggy meadow. The meadow was not large, just big enough to picket a horse or two. At the far end, I saw a large gray form in the shadows. My mind clicked: a canvas wall tent. Someone's base camp. Behind that, I saw movement. Packhorses. All right, I thought, a trail crew. They're here to sort out this mess and reopen the trail. They'll enjoy a little company. They will know the best way out of here and will have the route cleared. It will be smooth hiking from here.

I turned and took four long strides toward the wall tent. Then I stopped. My eyes screwed into focus. The wall tent, as if at some sorcerer's command, materialized into a granite boulder. A glacial erratic, capped with moss. There was no base camp. There was no trail crew or packhorses. I had hallucinated the whole thing.

"Ho-lee shit," I whispered. I shrugged out of my pack and let it thump to the ground.

"What?" Karen asked. "What is it?"

"I . . . uh . . . I like this meadow. Let's camp here. I think we've hiked far enough for one day."

"I don't know," Karen said. "It's pretty damp. Maybe we'll hit the main trail a little farther down. We still have a little light. Let's keep going."

But I already had the tent out of my pack and was flipping it across the grass. We would have to pitch it fast, as a fortress against the mosquitoes. Karen was too tired to protest. The tent sprouted like a blue mushroom. Karen crawled inside to peel off her muddy socks. I walked the edge of the meadow. Under a spruce tree, I noticed a place where a bear had made a daybed, probably that afternoon. I could see the scratches in the duff where he had scraped out the sticks to get to the soft earth. It was about fifteen feet from our tent. I shook my head, recalling our sleepless night on Mount Aeneas. I looked around, unzipped my fly, and pissed on the bear bed.

"I lay claim to this little meadow," I said. I zipped up, returned to the tent and peeled off my own muddy socks. We ate a cold dinner of trail mix and dried fruit and water.

"Who were you talking to?" Karen asked.

"No one," I said. I didn't mention the illusory wall tent, either. That could wait until morning.

EVEN WHEN BUD MOORE'S BODY was in Washington, D. C., his soul remained out West. Eventually, Moore was transferred back to Missoula. During the 1960s and '70s, he was in charge of fire management and operations for the Forest Service for northern Idaho, all of Montana, and parts of Washington and the Dakotas. But unlike most bureaucrats, Moore refused to stay behind his desk. At home he tended big pack dogs and at every opportunity he loaded their packsacks and disappeared for weeks at a time into the wilderness. In winter, he ran long traplines on snowshoes. There he contemplated the ageless cycles of birth, death, and rebirth. He saw the elk wintering in the brushy draws left by old forest fires. He noted that Lewis and Clark had nearly starved along the Lolo Trail for lack of elk. He watched the elk herds decline as the brush gradually grew again into dark timber. In unburned forests, Bud saw where the dead and decaying wood was stacking up and drying out. He knew that someday, the woods here would burn again, and there would not be a damn thing that he or any other mortal would be able to do about it.

Gradually, under the guidance of leaders like Moore, the Forest Service came to replace its militancy against fire with a kind of diplomacy. In most forests, the trees were simply too valuable as lumber to allow them to burn. In timber country and near cities and towns, Forest Service firefighters remained committed to snuffing forest fires before they grew too destructive. But in wilderness areas such as the Selway-Bitterroot, it made both ecological and economic sense to allow some fires to run their natural course. The Selway-Bitterroot Wilderness was one of the few places large and wild enough to be allowed its natural fires.

In short, Moore championed a strategy of living alongside natural processes instead of trying to bend them to human will. This was the logic of the land. The evidence was there. On the wing of Clark's nutcracker and the cone of the whitebark pine.

IT IS NO COINCIDENCE that the journals of Lewis and Clark record Clark's nutcracker and whitebark pine within days of each other. The bird and tree are intertwined. Whitebark pine seeds are unusually fat, caloric, and rich in protein. They are strictly a mountain tree, thriving at the highest altitudes. Their strong roots somehow seek out soil in this rocky ground, gripping boulders like an eagle's talons, holding firm through a thousand winters of mountain storms. The cones are tough and pitchy. They grow in clusters at the top of the pine's upswept limbs.

The Clark's nutcracker cracks the tough cones. It collects scores of the seeds in its gullet. Then the bird flies off, caching the seeds in the ground. A single nutcracker can stash 100,000 seeds in 15,000 caches. In one burn in Utah, Clark's nutcrackers cached 13,600 pine seeds per acre of forest. The bird reclaims some of these seeds, and animals from squirrels to grizzly bears eat many more. But enough seeds survive to germinate and sprout into the next generation of whitebark pines. It so happens that nutcrackers prefer to cache their seeds in sunny slopes, particularly in the ashes left by fire. Whitebark pines thrive under such cultivation. And so, this contract has held firm on these mountains for thousands of years. The agreement benefits all signatories—the bird, the pine, and the fire.

After decades of firefighting, the whitebark pine is unwell. Whitebark stands are commonly called ghost forests. Dead, brittle trees stand by the hundreds. From a distance, the mountain slopes appear grizzled with a gray beard of dead trees. In the dry mountain air, the skeleton trunks rot slowly, standing debarked and naked against the thin alpine sky. You have to search hard for even a single living sapling, and often one cannot be found at all.

Living whitebark pines often display great streamers of pitch on their trunk, like sticky tears. The needles are often faded a crisp, sickly red. These are signs of blister rust, an exotic fungus introduced to North America by European pines imported to a Canadian nursery. By coincidence, the disease was imported in 1910, the same year as the Great Burn. This disease has devastated whitebark pines throughout the northern Rockies and is still spreading. Even the relatively pristine, officially protected Selway-Bitterroot Wilderness cannot escape the changes brought by humans.

In Idaho and Montana, the whitebark pine has been reduced to 5 to 10 percent of its historic range. The pine is functionally extinct in many ranges. Farther south, in the highlands of Yellowstone National Park, the Wind River Range, and the Beartooth Plateau, one can see great stands of healthy whitebark pines and boisterous flocks of nutcrackers. However, blister rust is creeping gradually south.

As devastating as blister rust is, the tree might stand a chance, were it not for the absence of fire. Even if a few pines survive the disease, they cannot reproduce in the shade of dense, unburned forests. Moore and others like him knew that, without fire, the forest would choke out whitebark and other pines. They knew that fire belonged in the Bitterroot Wilderness, as much as the nutcracker and the whitebark pine. Without fire, the Bitterroot was changed forever. They just had to convince the Forest Service. And the American people.

MORNING CAME LATE to our little camp. High ridges and tall timber threw up their arms against the sun. The meadow dripped with condensation. We shook dew from the tent and crammed it in my pack soaking wet.

With a new day ahead of us, Karen and I collected our thoughts. We studied my old topographic map, comparing the merging stream tributaries to the twists of the map's contour lines. We pieced moose trail with moose trail, searching for signs of the official human pathway. Eventually we found them: fallen logs that had once been sawn out of the trail's way; old blazes— hatchet marks chipped on the bark of trees—that delineate a route. The sawn logs were soft and mossy; none of the blazes were on living, green trees. It had been decades since anyone cleared this trail. The stream had jumped its track, wiping out segments of trail and forcing us to wade. But our route began to make sense.

Step by step, mile by mile, we clawed our way out of the dark canyon. Piece by piece, the trail became discernible. By afternoon, we stumbled across an honest-to-god footpath, complete with fresh blazes on living trees. Another few miles and we found a wooden sign pointing the way to our destination. The trail parted a meadow of sunlight and wildflowers, with a great fir rising from the middle. We flopped in the shade of the tree and took a siesta. Things were looking up.

After our break, we continued climbing. The timber thinned as we gained altitude. The trail led to a cirque—a cup carved in the side of a mountain by a glacier now gone. The cirque was dotted with a chain of glistening mountain lakes, polished and shining. I thought of Thoreau's theory, that lakes are the hand mirrors of God. Reflected in this mirror was Grave Peak, a great pyramid of granite boulders. Karen pointed out the tiny cupola on the summit: Grave Peak Lookout. The 1919 outpost of young Norman Maclean.

The country was such prime bear habitat that I spent a few moments scanning for bear tracks, but found nothing more than a few ant logs that had been busted up long before. In 1919, Norman Maclean watched a grizzly from Grave Peak. But the bear lost to the sheepherders and gold prospectors. The last official record of a grizzly in the Bitterroots came in 1946, when a Forest Service ranger recorded grizzly tracks in the mud near Spruce Creek. That ranger was Bud Moore.

Our weariness fell behind us as we shed our backpacks. We enjoyed that odd, walking-on-air feeling that comes with dropping a burden one has carried for hours. We left our clothes in little piles on the lakeshore and waded into the cold, breath-taking water. We waded in to crotch level, then held our breath and dove into the lake's surface. We broke again into the sunshine, gasping for oxygen and shaking water from our heads. Echoes of our laughter bounced off the mountains. The atmosphere is thinner at a mile and a half above sea level, and the sun burns with extra strength. Large, flat boulders glimmered in the sun. We climbed on them and let the sun dry our naked bodies. Happy to be alive. Just happy.

We ate supper on the lakeshore, talking gently and easily. A breeze kept mosquitoes at bay. Trout rose on the water, but we were in a peaceable mood and were happy to let the fish feed. When dark came, we crashed asleep. I awoke in the tent in the middle of the night. I heard a great splashing outside. Karen grabbed my forearm. Criminy, I thought, we camped next to the last remaining grizzly bear in the Selway-Bitterroot. And by the sounds of it, one that enjoys a midnight skinny-dip.

Karen slowly unzipped the tent flap. The night air was chill outside the cozy loft of our sleeping bags. The starscape blazed overhead, the night sky moonless but fully a-dazzle with the suns of our galaxy. Grave Peak glistened crisp and eerie against the void, like a photo-negative of a mountain. The lake surface was the color of mercury, but it rippled in spite of the absolute stillness of the night. I squinted toward the sound.

"What is it?" I asked.

"There," Karen said, pointing. "I can see something moving across the lake."

There was the mysterious creature's head, followed by a quicksilver wake. Finally, the being arrived at shallow water and its immense black body rose up, sheeting water. I saw its legs grow, then its head silhouetted against the sky. I noticed antlers. It was a creature that Lewis and Clark glimpsed, but were never able to collect or prove existed to any scientific standard: *Alces alces.* A moose.

NORMAN MACLEAN AND BUD MOORE became fast friends, even after that stormy encounter over Maclean's manuscript. Maclean would visit Moore's cabin, with a fly rod in one hand and a Mason jar of whiskey in the other. Maclean would forget his hat upon leaving, providing a handy excuse for another visit. Eventually, Maclean's manuscript found a publisher and critical and financial success. Years later, after Maclean was famous, a reporter from *Esquire* magazine came to Montana for an interview. Maclean took the journalist straight to Moore's cabin. After *A River Runs Through It*, Maclean began to write his second book, *Young Men and Fire.* That book tells the tragedy of the squadron of smoke jumpers killed in the Mann Gulch fire in 1949. In the 1950s, the story had been a B-grade movie, *Red Skies Over Montana.* Maclean longed to give the story its literary due. Bud knew the story intimately and Norman told it immaculately, although the book was not published until after his death.

Their partnership was a sort of literary mutualism. Maclean supplied the literary genius, but Moore kept the author's feet in the ashen earth. But upon rereading the book, it struck me how differently the two men viewed this force, wildfire. Maclean was strictly old-school. He had in fire what every writer of heroic epics needs: an enemy of undoubtable evil. To him, the fight against fire was a noble battle. His fire is the fire of literature—a destructive god, a pestilence that chokes out life's very air, the enemy not only of man but of life itself.

Moore's view was something different. Something born of these mountains. Moore knew that fire could be a destructive force. He saw the homesteads left in cinder and knew the scorched-hair smell of cattle burned alive. But he also knew fire's creative force. He knew the whitebark pine, the Clark's nutcracker, and their story of natural mutualism. Moore, the unschooled trapper, backwoods ranger, reluctant bureaucrat, saw what was happening. His vision of fire—that it was neither pure enemy nor pure friend, but both—ran square into the entrenched dogma held by the Forest Service. But Moore and a handful of other visionaries kept swinging away at that dogma. Eventually they were able to turn the great war machine. They did not turn it completely around, but at least in a new direction. In places like the Selway-Bitterroot Wilderness, the Forest Service lets some lightning strikes go. It lets some fires burn.

This shift is akin to the philosophy that wishes grizzly bears to roam free, or rivers to run undammed and unregulated. If not everywhere, at least in what precious few wild places still have room for natural processes. Norman Maclean put it this way:

"The power of fire is so multiform that it often seems contradictory, and so the fires of hell are the symbol of humanity's passion, hate and eternal damnation, and the 'eternal flame' is the symbol of our hope for eternal peace and salvation."

Bud Moore's fire was something else again. It was not symbolic, but as real as the charred, insect-riddled snag that feeds the black-backed woodpecker. As actual as the corky, butterscotch-smelling bark of the ponderosa pine that allows the monarch tree to live for centuries as fires swirl around it. The whitebark pine both perishes and sprouts under fire. For the whitebark, the forces of death and of life are one single force, not competing ones. It remains to be seen if the new vision has come in time to save the whitebark.

THE MORNING AFTER THE MOOSE, Karen and I reluctantly broke camp. We swung into our packs and climbed out of the cirque. We crested Friday Pass, on the southern flank of Grave Peak. We were greeted with a sight similar to those of the days of Lewis and Clark: an ocean of rock rolling out to the horizon. All around us arose jagged mountain after jagged mountain, in a dozen shades of hazy blue.

We dropped our packs and soaked in this sight. Mountain lakes glistened hundreds of feet below us, their bottoms clearly visible even from this height. I scanned the horizon. Nowhere could I see a road, a clear-cut, a mine, a building. It looked like the dawn of time. The only sign of people was the trail leading to the old lookout atop Grave Peak.

"Look there," Karen said, pointing in the air below us. "Nutcracker." A Clark's nutcracker flew past. Karen tracked it with her binoculars. The bird landed atop a tree. Sure enough, a whitebark pine. The bird bent its head and stabbed at the pine cones at the top of the crown. It would stab the cone, four or five times, and then pause to take the seeds into its throat.

I examined the tree itself. It was a stout, mature citizen in seemingly perfect health. Only then did I notice another nutcracker, and another. And another pine. And another. There were saplings, small trees and mature ones. We were standing over a small grove of whitebark. The trees were vibrant green, with no seeping wounds on their trunks and no dead needles. Perhaps these trees had the secret gene that had helped them survive the blister rust epidemic. Perhaps this stand was a reservoir of hope. We watched the birds gorge. Soon their throats bulged with collected seeds. One by one, they launched from the treetops, looking for some open space to cache their stash.

Thus cheered, Karen and I pulled our packs back on. We could make a couple more miles by evening, if we kept moving. I took a long look around at the frozen ocean of granite sweeping away on all sides. Over to the south, deep in the wilderness, I noticed something for the first time: a small plume of smoke. Somewhere, a fire burned.

Chapter 9

Playing God with God's Dog

WOLF
Canis lupus
COYOTE
Canis latrans

"HOW ARE YOU IN SMALL AIRPLANES?" DAVE HOERNER asked, his eyes hidden behind the saturated tint of aviation glasses.

Truth is, I've never trusted the damn things. I dislike the way small planes bounce against the wind, straining the rivets with every drop in altitude. When I worked as a newspaper reporter, I sometimes walked through the wreckage of small airplane crashes, pondering motorized flight as the dead pilot's notes, maps, and charts blew uselessly around my feet. So I tried to play casual.

"I haven't thrown up in one yet," I replied.

Hoerner smiled behind his headset microphone. "We could change that today, if you like," he said.

"No thanks," I said. "But do you have a bag handy, just in case?"

"Here's what you do," Hoerner said. "Move your eyes, but not your head. If you move your head, it messes with your inner ears. That's where the vertigo comes from. Just hold your head still and look with your eyes. You'll be fine."

From this altitude, the snowy landscape looked dwarfed and distant. A winter forest spread out below us, like a map of itself. To the east, mountain ranges rippled one after another; the hostile mass of rock to the east marked the Continental Divide. The Blackfeet called these mountains the Backbone of the World. On the western horizon was the diminutive but equally rugged Cabinet Range. The cordilleras appeared as impenetrable fortresses of ice and rock. A black thread of asphalt—U.S. Highway 93—ran north-south like the Continental Divide itself, from Mexico to Canada and beyond.

Invisible in the mountains, white goats clung to wind-scoured crags. Bears slumbered thickly in their winter dens. The elk and deer that summer in the mountains were wintering directly below us, where the forest was relatively gentle. Since the elk and deer were down low, so were the wolves.

Wolves are controversial enough in the modern West that

people want to know where they are and where they might be headed. That's Hoerner's job, to keep tabs on the packs recolonizing the Rockies. We were flying in late winter, a few weeks before the wolves' mating season. Wolves will rove hundreds of miles during this season—crossing mountains, rivers, freeways—looking for a mate or just wandering about. The wolves were somewhere in the forest below. Scattered over hundreds of square miles were six packs, ranging in size from two to a dozen animals. They were wired for sound. One Judas wolf in each pack wore a radio collar. Each wing on Hoerner's overbuilt Cessna was equipped with a radio antenna. Once within radio range of the wolves, Hoerner simply tilted the plane toward the beep and, as if by drawn by some shaman's spell, we would arrive at the pack.

It was my old wolf-tracking friend Mike Fairchild who introduced me to Hoerner. "He's the best," Mike said. "That's all there is to it."

Hoerner used to work with biologists like Fairchild in the cockpit most of the time. The biologists did the looking, while Hoerner did the flying. Even so, Hoerner usually spotted the wolf first. Eventually it dawned on the government bean-counters that Hoerner was perfectly good at both jobs and the government could save money hiring Hoerner alone. So now the biologists work on the ground and Hoerner flies after the wolves. Once the wolves are located, he receives the coordinates from a global positioning system receiver. Back at the office, he sends the data to authorities via the Internet. If the wolves are near a cattle herd, he will give the rancher a telephone call.

The peregrinations of wolves are wonderful to behold. A female numbered B-45 once left the comfortable wilds of central Idaho and crossed Hells Canyon, swam the Snake River, to poke around in Oregon. A wolf tagged in Montana was shot along the Peace River in northern Alberta, and might have made it to the Yukon had her luck been better. Nature is full of these stories: arctic owls that show up in Texas; a Montana elk that wandered to Missouri; a mountain lion in Michigan. The instinct to explore is not the sole property of humans. Curiosity may have killed a cat or two, but it rewarded many more with a meal and a mate.

So we searched for the wolves. Big Brother aboard a Cessna. I was a little torn in my mind, searching for wolves like this. I was unsettled by the dead-on certainty of it. On one hand, I couldn't deny the excitement of seeking wild wolves. On the other, swooping down on wolves like some demigod was entirely different from *encountering* wolves. I felt like a cheat, but couldn't help enjoying it.

"Have you ever seen a wolf before?" Hoerner asked, making conversation as we flew.

"A few," I answered, silently recalling them. There was the bushy-tailed black wolf that Karen and I kicked out of a cottonwood grove, dry leaves flying in its wake as it fled. Another wolf, a salt-and-pepper beast on a misty May evening, trotted over a sagebrush flat and turned its thick muzzle toward me before melting into the timber. There was that pair of pointed ears poking from a long-grass meadow that, upon closer inspection, turned into a heavy-shouldered gray, and then another and another, until the entire pack was loping across the glade.

Then there were the wolves I never did see, perhaps more vivid in my memory than the visible animals. The wolf that left the fresh-this-morning tracks on a frozen river in Alberta. I followed the trail for a long March day on my skis, never seeing its creator.

Another winter, as Karen and I skied in Montana's North Fork of the Flathead Valley. We had skied six miles to our camp, breaking trail all the way, before digging a snow cave. As we slept, a wolf pack used our ski trail as an easy route through the mountains. The next day, it was our turn to ski over their tracks.

I recalled the torrential weekend Karen and I paddled a kayak the length of Kintla Lake, just one ridge south of Canada. It rained like Montana had a monsoon season. We camped early, the rain plastering our tent. We crawled naked into the sleeping bags, our clothes a sodden heap at our feet. The mountain was so saturated that throughout the night, landslides crashed off the slopes and into the lake. Past midnight, I awoke in utter darkness and heard that the rain had stopped. There was only the slow sprinkle of water dripping off the fir boughs, the smell of wet forest and moist loam.

Then, I heard them. At first just a low, throaty bay that rose like a distant siren. The sound hung in the thick, moist air for a long moment, just disappearing before it was answered by another, then another, and then the wolfen chorus blending so there was no individual voice but only the song of the pack. Then they went silent. I touched Karen and she awoke.

"Listen," I whispered. And in a moment we heard the animals echo each other once again.

"Wolves," Karen said. It was so dark I could not see her face, but I swear I could hear her smile.

WOLVES WERE NOTHING NEW—and certainly nothing romantic—to the men of the Lewis and Clark Expedition. The explorers had known wolves in the Atlantic states. They judged the Great Plains wolves to be slightly smaller than those back home and they were probably right.

A walk in any city park illustrates that dogs are America's favorite animal. Dogs are simply small wolves. All our domestic variants are wolves that our selective breeding has morphed into fuzzy, friendly, sheep-herding, bird-pointing, and lap-sitting mutants. Your neighbor's neurotic Pomeranian may look like a rodent, but it's a wolf, twisted around human desire. Yet, if domestic dogs are America's favorite animal, their wild brethren are near the other end of the pole. Around A.D. 1200, St. Francis of Assisi called wolves "brothers." But that never really caught on. To most Europeans, wolves were basically Satan in a fur suit. England destroyed the last of its wolves in the 1700s. In the New World, the newly independent colonists set to duplicate that score in North America.

In the New World, wolves lived everywhere American Indians did. These people saw wolves in a fundamentally different light than Europeans did. Wolves and Indians were both hunters, and the natives admired the wolf's cunning, endurance, and toughness. According to some anthropologists, early humans learned cooperative hunting tactics by watching wolves. Indeed, Lewis and Clark noted that wolves and Indian horsemen hunted the pronghorn in the same manner: chasing the swift creatures in relays, tag-teaming each other until the prey was exhausted.

North American Indians did not domesticate feral Spanish horses until around 1720. For thousands of years before that, Indians subjugated dogs as beasts of burden. In the northern Great Plains, tamed wolves toted travois, A-shaped drag sticks with a person's belongings tied aboard. The line between domestic and wild wolf was blurry. While Indians occasionally killed a wolf for a pelt, they saw the animal more as a brother hunter than as a threatening competitor. Wolves were handy to have around: Their keen senses might alert an observant hunter to game or to danger.

Lewis and Clark found wolves both abundant and relatively tame. In Kansas they watched a wolf lolling on a sandbar, oddly near a flock of wild turkeys. Early in the expedition, Pvt. Reuben Fields captured a wolf pup and attempted to tame it. The whelp chewed through its leather rope and escaped, depriving the expedition of a unique mascot. During the long, hungry crossing of the Lolo Trail, the expedition heard wolves howl at night, a sound that must have only exacerbated their lonesomeness.

Lewis and Clark found wolves wherever big game was abundant. Along the Missouri, wolves troubled the expedition's hunters. Scouts foraged ahead of the main group, shooting deer, elk, or bison and leaving the meat where the crew would find it. Wolves frequently devoured cached venison before the expedition reached it.

In May 1805, while walking up the Missouri River in north-central Montana, the expedition passed the massive heap of drowned bison left ashore by the spring floods at the mouth of what they called the Slaughter River. Wolves feasted on the fetid carcasses and loafed around, bellies bloated with meat. "The wolves are fat and extreemly gentle," Clark noted. One wolf was so complacent that Clark walked within a few feet and impaled it with his espontoon, a fancy spear carried by the officers.

The wolves were not always gentle. On the homeward journey of 1806, the Corps split into two teams. Clark's party descended the Yellowstone River, eventually regrouping with Lewis in what is now North Dakota. Clark tells of the Yellowstone country that July:

"For me to mention or give estimate of the different species of animals in this river, particularly Buffalow, Antelope and Wolves, would be incredible. I shall therefore be silent on the subject farther."

But in early August, wolves revisited Clark's journal. The band's horses had been stolen by Crow Indians. The men were camped along the Yellowstone, not far from the future site of Billings, Montana. According to Clark's journal, a lone wolf stole into camp at night and bit Sgt. John Pryor "through the hand" while the man slept. The wolf turned on Pvt. Richard Windsor before a third man shot the beast. Clark called the wolf "vicious," but gave no indication that it might be rabid, starving, or otherwise ill.

This is remarkably unusual behavior for a wolf. The *Audubon Society Field Guide to Mammals* says there have been only three documented wild wolf attacks on the continent. Clark offers no explanation. My own speculation is that the wolf was a semi-tamed wolf-slave of the nearby Indians, perhaps driven out of camp for its ill temper. The animal may have associated campfires with food and wandered in for a handout. Or maybe Clark's patrol just crossed a wolf with a bad attitude.

That same summer, Lewis ventured far to the north of Clark, exploring the Sun and Teton Rivers in the land of the Blackfeet. This remains a dramatic landscape, the Rocky Mountain Front, where the mountains stack up as one jagged range behind the other, rising abruptly from the plain. Black thunderclouds roar down from the peaks to gallop across the prairie. Brutal winds rip road signs in half and derail freight trains. The tracings of Blackfeet travois trails are still etched on the rangeland here, amid the oil derricks and cow dung. It is cattle country, through and through. But when Lewis visited, the land teemed with bison.

"Immense and numerous herds of the buffaloe and their scarcely less numerous sheepherds, the wolves," Lewis wrote. Along the Sun River, he wrote of wolves running in "vast assembleges."

Wolves hunt bison in large packs, running in long, extended attacks. Pursuits can last days as wolves harry and bite at their targets, ripping haunches until the stiff, exhausted animals turn and make a feeble final stand. In Alberta, wolves have been clocked attacking bison eleven hours at a stretch, covering fifty miles overnight. But between these chases, the predator and prey maintain an uneasy truce, wolves and bison mingling in apparent unconcern until some secret signal triggers another pursuit.

On the Rocky Mountain Front, the bison are gone, replaced in the 1880s by bovines that may be driven to Chicago slaughterhouses instead of driven off cliffs. Wolves turned to cattle, and ranchers responded with poison, bullets, and traps. By the 1930s, wolves were essentially gone, not only from the Rocky Mountain Front, but from virtually every other corner of the American West.

But wolves are making a comeback. A few have made it back to the Rocky Mountain Front. Hoerner tells the story as we fly.

In 1988, wolf researcher Diane Boyd was working in the Wigwam River drainage, just north of the Canadian line in the province of British Columbia. The Wigwam Valley is winter range for deer, elk, and bighorn sheep and Boyd suspected it was a launching pad for wolves striking south to recolonize the United States. A robust pack had survived there for several winters and Boyd wanted to know where they were going and what they were up to.

That summer, Boyd caught a thirty-one-pound, three-month-old pup in a steel trap. Diane didn't even have to drug the wolf—just grabbed its neck and wrestled the whelp into submission. The wolf was so small a radio collar would have promptly fallen off. So Diane snapped yellow plastic tags on its ears and set the animal free. The pup was logged as No. 8808.

The year after Boyd tagged the pup, the Wigwam pack mysteriously disappeared. Boyd's track surveys turned up no wolf sign in the Wigwam. Sketchy evidence suggested a vandal poisoned the lot of them. Boyd searched for the vanished wolves, but eventually gave them up for dead.

Now the story skips ahead, to a different decade and country. It is February 1993. The setting is the Rocky Mountain Front of Montana, 150 miles southeast of the lush forests of British Columbia. Specifically the Sun River, where Lewis noted those "vast assembledges" of wolves in 1806. But there had not been a wolf here since 1930.

The Montana Department of Fish, Wildlife and Parks maintains a winter range at the headwaters of the Sun, where elk congregate by the hundreds. In February 1993, a game warden and maintenance worker were on patrol, checking the Sun River Game Range for trespass and mending fence. They found a set of large paw prints in the shallow snow, diamond-shaped like a coyote's, but much larger. Instinctively they took up the trail. They topped a ridge and saw before them a pair of wolves, standing over a calf elk so recently killed that the torn carcass gave up steam. Two wolves—one large gray and a somewhat smaller black—saw the men and fled.

The wolf sighting caused a stir in the nearby ranch town of Augusta. State and federal wildlife authorities secured a helicopter and within hours were on the trail of the wolves. The dark female escaped, but the gunner was able to shoot the big gray in the haunch with a tranquilizer dart.

As the animal sagged under the drug, the men landed and prepared to radio-collar the wolf. Upon approaching the downed animal, the first thing they noted was the size of their specimen. The wolf weighed 121 pounds. (My field guide to mammals puts the top weight for gray wolves at 120 pounds.) The wolf had a gray back, with white legs and face, and a gray fringe around the ears and muzzle. The men put a radio collar around the wolf's massive neck and prepared to plug a tag in its ear. Then they saw that the wolf already wore yellow plastic ear tags.

It was wolf 8808, the scrawny pup Diane Boyd had trapped in British Columbia. Wolf 8808 was the only known survivor of the Wigwam pack. He had survived the suspected poisoning, traveled nearly two hundred miles, crossed several major rivers, crested the Continental Divide, and skipped across an international boundary. Somehow, in this vast, nearly wolfless range, he had found a mate. Together the pioneering pair were staking out the new, eastern border of Rocky Mountain wolf range. "It was a situation that was too good to be true," Boyd told me later.

Later that spring, the wolf's radio signal led authorities to the spot on a nearby ranch where the wolves had dug a den in the earth. The place was thick with elk in winter and whitetail deer all year round. But cattle bellowed within earshot. Ranchers would not tolerate depredation of their stock. If the wolves were to survive, they would need self-restraint. And luck.

Hoerner was there, with his airplane and that omniscient radio receiver. He periodically dropped in on the pack from the air, while other agents checked in from the ground. Locally the pair was dubbed Bonnie and Clyde. The wag who picked that name no doubt suspected trouble would be forthcoming.

Bonnie and Clyde kept their muzzles clean for one year, then two. The pair grew into a pack. They roamed in pursuit of elk and deer, then returned to the den to regurgitate venison for their clamoring pups. The clowning, teething pups chewed the radio collar off Clyde's neck. Biologists trapped another pack member, fixing another radio on it. The biologists, the ranchers, and the local hunting guides all kept their eyes on the wolves.

The pack's luck ran cold. A hard winter in 1996 drove down the local population of deer. Faced with another hungry litter of pups, two members of the Sun River pack killed a cow. Then a calf. The wolves had crossed a line visible to ranchers and bureaucrats, but invisible to wolves. The ranchers had tolerated the wolves thus far, but could not afford repeated depredations. The old range war was resparked.

The federal agriculture agents were called in with their steel traps and helicopter gunmen. First, two wolves were trapped, hauled by pickup to distant mountains and set free. The banished pair fared poorly. One was shot surreptitiously. The other, injured in the initial capture, was unable to survive in the strange territory.

Meanwhile, the remaining pack hunted amid the cattle. Watching the Sun River pack was like watching an alcoholic who had sworn off booze but works in a liquor store. Temptation was all around. Over several months the pack killed only natural prey. But the beef proved irresistible and the pack returned to kill cattle.

Finally, Hoerner was called in for one last mission. He pinpointed the pack from the air, calling their coordinates by radio. A helicopter flew in behind and below him. The gunner hung out the open helicopter door by a waist belt, his 12-gauge shotgun loaded with buckshot. The offspring of Bonnie and Clyde were systematically gunned down.

"It's a hell of a thing," Hoerner said. "Here I had watched the wolves for years, seen them raise pups and survive. Then, it was my job to help clean them out."

Clyde himself, old No. 8808, escaped the gunning. He was never captured again. Some believe he was shot and stuffed down a badger hole by an angry rancher or jealous elk hunter. Some think he may have taken cover in the rugged mountains to the west. Some think the wolf with yellow plastic ear tags may someday show up again. Cattlemen still see the odd wolf on the Rocky Mountain Front. The tracks of lone animals are sometimes found after a fresh snowfall. Wolves have attempted to reclaim the Sun River country, but each time have run afoul of ranchers and have been destroyed.

"Wolves on the Rocky Mountain Front are just going to have a real hard time surviving," federal biologist Joe Fontaine told me. "There's not enough wild prey compared to the number of livestock. Wolves may come again. They may den and survive a year or two, but I just don't see them holding on for long."

The shotgun blasts closed another chapter in an old story. A story that is still unfolding across the continent. Unfolding in ways we never imagined.

LEWIS AND CLARK knew about wolves before leaving home. But the explorers knew nothing of the wolf's smaller cousin, *Canis latrans.* The coyote.

From an evolutionary standpoint, the plains of North America were the source of the world's canids, not unlike the savannas of Africa were later the source of the world's hominids. Coyotes have roamed North America for roughly 3 million years and have stuck to the continent. Wolves are a younger species, a specialized canid that evolved later to hunt the large prey mammals that it followed throughout Europe, Asia, and North America.

There is no clear note in the journals about where Lewis and Clark saw their first coyote. Initially the explorers mistook coyotes for the familiar gray fox. But finally in 1804, not without some difficulty, they shot a coyote on the plains of South Dakota. With a specimen in hand, they knew this was not a wolf, exactly, and not a fox, but a creature in-between. It was a new creature, unnamed in the English language. English borrowed the word *coyote* from Spanish, but the word is ultimately derived from the Aztec language of Nahuatl. *Coyote* translates to *the dog of the gods.* Lewis and Clark called it the "small wolf" or the "burrowing wolf of the prairie."

"They are active, fleet and delicately built," Lewis wrote. "The eye is of deep sea green colour, small and piercing."

Clark wrote: "The prairie wolf . . . barkes like a large ferce dog . . . They frequently salute us with this note as we pass through the plains."

Lewis and Clark presented the American Philosophical Society with the boiled bones of a coyote. Subsequently, Americans plastered their old mythology of wolves onto this new canid. If the wolf was Satan in fur, the coyote was a lesser breed of demon. Coyotes rarely attack cows, as do wolves, but they will slay sheep with vigor, especially during the lambing season. Lambs are the symbols of Christly innocence. Coyotes, well . . . coyotes are little wolves. Pioneering Americans fought wolf and coyote with the same weaponry: traps, bullets, coursing dogs. Those paled compared to biological warfare in the form of poison. Poisons clobbered American wolves by the 1930s. Strychnine and a later poison, Compound 1080, destroyed not only wolves, but also cougars, wolverines, and lynx, as ranchers and their governmental aides tried to make the West safe for livestock.

But coyotes survived. Coyotes are remarkably fecund creatures, sandwiched squarely in the middle of the food chain. When persecuted, they make up their losses by cranking out more pups. Females in heavily hunted or trapped populations double the size of their litters and a higher percentage of females breed. "If you kill one coyote," a biologist told me, "three more show up in its place. It's like bailing the ocean."

Americans have waged an incessant battle against coyotes, and this battle continues unabated. Today, the federal government alone kills eighty thousand annually. Add to that tens of thousands more killed by ranchers, varmint hunters, fur trappers, and automobiles. In ranch country, coyotes are shot reflexively. A rancher thinks as much about shooting a coyote as a suburbanite does about mowing the lawn. Just a job that needs being done.

Still, coyotes not only survive, but thrive. Coyotes are biological racquetballs: The harder we hit them, the higher they bounce back. After two centuries of relentless persecution, coyotes are more common and more widespread than ever before. There are probably more coyotes today than during the days of Lewis and Clark.

For all our wrath and technology, humans are ineffective predators on coyotes. Wolves, on the other hand, are hell on legs for coyotes. Wolves are always on the hunt, sniffing out competing coyotes and killing them. Consider Yellowstone National Park. In 1995, wolves were reintroduced after many a fifty-year absence. In the park's Lamar Valley, the number of coyotes dropped by 50 percent after wolves set up residence. Wolves not only out-compete coyotes for protein, they see the smaller dogs as trespassers in their territories. Wolves kill coyotes on sight, even digging coyote pups out of dens and shaking them like terriers do rats.

So when North America was full of wolves, it was not so full of coyotes. When colonists first arrived at the Atlantic seaboard, the newcomers immediately encountered their old nemesis, the wolf. But they did not encounter coyotes for two hundred years. The combined forces of the Mississippi River and the wolf kept coyotes confined to the western portion of the continent. Coyotes were in South Dakota, waiting for Lewis and Clark to stumble across them. And so in our imagination today, coyotes remain distinctly Western, like saguaro or sagebrush. But that, too, is changing.

WOLVES NEED RED MEAT and plenty of it. Forget what you saw about wolves living on mice in the movie *Never Cry Wolf.* Wolves eat about eight pounds of meat a day. Deer. Caribou. Bison. Elk. Cows. Sheep. The equation that eradicated American wolves is simple. Pioneers replaced the land's venison with beef and mutton. When wolves switched, they were exterminated. Coyotes, however, fit in the cracks. Coyotes squeak by on mice or rabbits, or even corn cobs and fallen apples if it comes down to it. Coyotes are cagey enough to live in the brushy edges of sub-urban Los Angeles, sneaking out at night to eat spilled trash or unwary house cats. That combination of street smarts and dietary flexibility gave coyotes an edge in agriculturalized and industrialized North America.

As Americans removed wolves, coyotes filled the void. By the 1930s, coyotes roamed the upper Midwest, where they had rarely been seen before. They moved into southern Canada. There something remarkable occurred. In the decades following World War II, predator control created a no-man's-land for wild dogs in southern Canada. Most of the wolves had been eradicated. But coyotes were only beginning to creep in. Late in the twentieth century, the eastern coyote trickled south from Ontario. They spread northward through Canada. In 1971 a coyote was killed at Riviere du Loup (Wolf River), Quebec. Years later, coyotes crossed the ice one cold winter to colonize Prince Edward Island.

South of Canada, hunters reported coyotes in New Jersey in 1948, and one was finally shot as proof in 1958. By 1960, coyotes spread south through Pennsylvania, feeding on fencerow rabbits and roadkill deer. They were big, robust specimens, fully a third larger than a typical coyote of the West. Some weighed nearly one hundred pounds—triple what a coyote of the Southwest might weigh. County by county, township by township, state by state, coyotes reclaimed the Northeast. In 1993 two coyotes were killed by cars in Delaware, and the species was thus confirmed there was well.

Meanwhile, coyotes swam across the Mississippi River, farther to the south. Coyotes were first recorded in the state of Mississippi in 1966. By 1988, the state had an estimated population of four hundred thousand coyotes. They spread to Alabama. From both north and south, the new coyotes filled the eastern seaboard. The eastern coyote crept through Virginia, haunting the outskirts of Jefferson's Monticello. Wise, nocturnal coyotes ghost through the suburbs of Washington, D.C. They raid watermelon patches in rural Florida.

Coyotes have blanketed the continent. East belongs to the coyote, as does the West. Today, every state except Hawaii is home to coyotes. By all estimates, the new coyotes are here to stay. But there is one telling detail about this new breed, the eastern coyote. Western coyotes are famous songsters. Their yodels and howls fill starry nights from desert to alpine heights. But common wisdom maintains that eastern coyotes hardly ever howl. The coyotes learned—or were perhaps unnaturally selected—to keep their mouths shut. They could not afford to arouse suspicions in this new land so dense with enemies. The new coyotes must maintain a low profile. They are explorers, claiming new territory.

MY HEADSET FILLED with a *ping*, heavy in the right phone, lighter in the left. It was steady and strong, as if the radio somehow transmitted the wolf's pulse. Hoerner canted the plane toward the sound. Toward the west and north. The volume increased as we flew steady into it.

"I need your eyes here," Hoerner said. "Keep them open."

The snowy forest rolled below us. I gazed out the window without moving my head, as Hoerner had instructed. I let Hoerner worry about finding the wolves. I worried about not losing my breakfast. Hoerner tilted his head for a better view and the plane tilted, too.

"They're down there, right below us," he said. Hoerner dropped the plane like a swooping eagle, reached the low point in the downward parabola, then pulled into a climbing spiral. The spiral was narrow at first, circles growing larger as we climbed, to avoid flying through the turbulence of our own prop wash. Then we dropped into another swoop, another dip, and another climb. I had one of Karen's spare cameras with a telephoto lens in my lap. I checked the film. I hooked a finger through the latch on the plane's window. The treetops sped past, uncomfortably near the landing gear. No wolves.

WOLVES AND COYOTES—like late spring blizzards, extended droughts, vegetarian cookbooks, and meatpacking monopolies—pose economic hardships for ranchers. Writer Barry Lopez said it well: You can't shoot a blizzard, but you can shoot a wolf. Today, western wolves are protected by federal law, but are frequently shot anyway. It's difficult to find—and even more difficult to convict—a wolf shooter in the modern West. I once attended a Montana Stock Growers meeting where the door prize was a .270-caliber rifle. The raffle tickets each had a picture of a wolf in a rifle's crosshairs.

Coyotes are still shot on sight in the West, out of frontier habit. They are left draped over barbed wire fences, like greasy fur coats tossed casually over the backs of chairs. This is perfectly legal. If anything, this habit probably just leads to more coyotes—the persecution stimulating greater reproduction.

But as new attitudes take over the West, wolves are regaining tenuous ground. Poisons like strychnine and Compound 1080 are controlled. Ranchers and others may not simply shoot wolves reflexively. Under protection of the Endangered Species

Act, wolves seem to be recolonizing western Montana and have been reintroduced to central Idaho and northwestern Wyoming. Some environmental groups have been willing to pay ranchers to compensate them for stock lost to wolves, and to help find ways to keep stock and wolves apart. Wolves are learning to live around humans, and humans are learning to live around wolves. But this new hand has just been dealt. The poker game is far from over.

We descended on a clear-cut. The plane's shadow raced over a field of snow and stumps. The clear-cut was stubbled with naked young larch. In the middle of the clear-cut was a patch of trees left standing in the leveled forest like crumbs left on a table. The signal was coming from the trees.

"Look in the trees," Hoerner said. "I've got them. Get ready."

Hoerner counted wolves. For the life of me, I could not see any.

Finally I spied one: a miniature wolf walking directly below us, through the trees. These wolves are not hunted from planes and paid us no mind. Once my eyes knew what to look for, they picked out another wolf and another. One sniffed at a splotch of red in the snow, another flopped in a patch of sunlight like an old hound on a porch.

"Get ready," Hoerner said, pushing forward with the controls, dropping the plane into a nauseating decline. "We're just going to do this once." The idea was to find the wolves, make one quick pass for an accurate count, then leave the creatures alone. I would only have one chance if I wanted a photograph. I twisted the latch on the window and opened it. The window opens from the bottom, held wide open by wind and centrifugal force. The cold wind blew my hair back, pushed my eyes into their sockets. The Nikon had no neck strap, so I clutched the body tight and pointed the lens out the window.

"We got 'em!" Hoerner said, banking the plane for a better view. "*Yee* ha! How many do you count?"

I thought: Now here is a man who enjoys his job. I squinted. On the far side of the trees, another wolf stood alone in the open snow. A black adult. I pointed the camera out the window. Hoerner tilted my side of the cockpit at the animal. The wolf turned its dark face toward the plane. A raven—the wolf's black partner—swept up from the timber and flew between the wolf and the plane.

I squinted through the viewfinder and found the wolf in the focus ring. I hit the shutter, advanced a frame, and snapped another shot before the plane swept over the wolf and took the animal out of view. Hoerner banked the plane. My stomach flipped between ribs. I turned my head and caught one more glimpse of the wolf as we regained altitude. The wolf and the raven continued on their way, like specks of soot on snow. Like black text on a white page. Like the sides of a Tao symbol. As if anything in nature, anything in the world, is black and white.

Chapter 10

The Fish Most Skookum

WHITE STURGEON
Acipenser transmontanus

I SAW THE PICTURES OF THE DINOSAUR IN A CAFE IN downtown Astoria, Oregon. The photograph was clipped from a newspaper and yellowed with age, but the image of the enormous creature still stopped me—the dinosaur was fresh-caught, with a man standing over it.

Astoria overlooks the Columbia River estuary, perched on the cusp of the continent. The Columbia River flows 1,245 miles from a narrow lake in the Canadian Rockies to meet its maker, the Pacific Ocean, at Astoria. Rain clouds rise from the ocean, washing inland to perpetually dampen the Pacific Northwest. Astoria sits on the cutting edge of the hydrologic cycle and catches the brunt of it. Rain defines Astoria the way sun defines Phoenix. Astoria receives five feet of precipitation annually. All of it rain.

Karen and I found Astoria quaint in the way rural Oregonians resent being called quaint: the working wharf, with its peeling paint, tugboats, and piscine odors; hills thick with fern, alder, and blackberry. The homes were Victorian and Craftsman in style and the downtown charming with classic stonemasonry.

We arrived in mid-deluge. The gutters on Marine Avenue ran like rivers and the atmosphere was mostly liquid. Astorians walked about with no trace of hurry. I suspected that if one removed an Astorian's galoshes, one might find webbed feet.

We folded sections of the *Oregonian* overhead and ran for cover. We ordered tea and donuts in a little side-street cafe that smelled of Folger's coffee and looked like a picture from an old *Life* magazine. Karen unfolded the sodden paper on the table and tried to decipher the smeared ink.

Outside the cafe, the Columbia spread expansively, forming the watery reach between Washington and Oregon. To the west, the misty line between sky and ocean was lost in gray. A bridge connected Oregon and Washington, four miles long and so high it appeared science-fictional, like a landing ramp for alien space-craft. Freighters passed under the bridge on the way to inland ports, full of televisions from Japan, or pointed back toward the ocean with a load of grain for Korean noodles. Three super-tankers were moored offshore.

The mouth of the Columbia River was the turnaround point for the Corps of Discovery. They had achieved their goal and just needed to wait out another winter and return safely home. Here, they were as far from home as any of them would ever be. They had crossed the entire continent by foot, horse, and boat. Roughly four thousand miles so far.

"Ocian in View!" Clark wrote nearby. "O the joy!"

Then they made the beach. And the rain hit.

"O! How horriable is the day," Clark wrote a few days later.

No coffee shops for him.

Even before the Corps arrived, the mouth of the Columbia was in the grasp of the global economy. Sea otter pelts, luxurious beyond all others, were free for the skinning and in high demand in Canton and other Chinese ports. Russian, British, and Spanish entrepreneurs were cashing in and Americans wanted a piece of the action. When Lewis and Clark met the local Clatsop Indians, they found them already schooled in international commerce. The phrase "son of a bitch" was rooted in the local vocabulary. The explorers had depleted their trade goods during their journey, putting them at another disadvantage in the local marketplace. A full day's bartering with the shrewd Clatsop might result in a handful of roots.

For Lewis and Clark, the winter of 1805–06 was a prison sentence of rain and tedium. In four months at Fort Clatsop, only twelve days were dry. Rain poured. It drizzled. It misted. That winter was inordinately wet, even for this soggy climate. The Corps suffered through a monotonous, miserable winter, their store of elk meat moldering as they ate it, their leather clothing rotting off their backs, inescapable fleas gradually driving them buggy.

Still, the estuary of the Columbia was an amazing sight. Estuaries—the places where freshwater meets salt—are the most fecund locations on Earth. Half the living mass of the world's oceans come from estuaries. The larger the estuary, the more life it supports, and the Columbia is one of the largest. The mouth of the Columbia River was even more biologically rich than the cold, arid Great Plains.

In the fall, geese, ducks, and swans gathered by the hundreds of thousands. They kept the explorers awake all night with their "horrid" ruckus. The waters were rich with plankton, microorganisms feeding everything from candlefish to baleen whales. Pods of sea otters and harbor seals bobbed in the black water. The shore was virtually impenetrable with Sitka spruce and Douglas fir—trees centuries old and six or seven feet thick, towering more than two hundred feet overhead. Herds of oversize Roosevelt elk tramped through the forests, moving silently over the mossy forest floor. Giant blue whales were stranded ashore, scavenged by the enormous California condors and washed by the incessant waves.

The Pacific Ocean here is notoriously un-pacific. In the two hundred years since Lewis and Clark, some two thousand ships have wrecked in this graveyard of the Pacific. Today, the rusty, barnacle-encrusted skeletons of wrecked steamers dissolve slowly on the beaches. U.S. Coast Guard specialists train here to perform rescues in hurricane seas. But in the 1800s, expert Clatsop boatmen plied these waters in elaborate canoes carved out of cedar logs. In a feat of remarkable daring, the Corps paddled their own hollowed logs across the broad mouth of the Columbia, getting seasick in the swells.

Upon their arrival, Clark led a small expedition to view the ocean. They followed the river's north shore to a rocky point now called Cape Disappointment, Washington. There, Clark noted a remarkable fish. The creature had washed a shore, or perhaps was stranded by an ebbing tide. Clark paced it off and recorded that the fish was ten feet long.

It was *Acipenser transmontanus,* the Columbia River white sturgeon. I wonder if expedition fisherman Silas Goodrich flipped at news of this discovery.

Later, Lewis described in detail how the Indians prepared the fish by steaming it. First they dug a trench, building a fire in the bottom. They laid rocks over a bed of coals, layering fish meat and fir boughs over the rocks. Then they would pour water on the rocks, producing enough steam to cook the fish.

"Prepared this way, sturgeon is better than boiled or roasted," Lewis wrote. And no doubt a pleasant break from rank elk.

Karen and I, on the other hand, split a donut in the little cafe in Astoria. The rain didn't stop as we sipped our tea, but finally did let up a bit. Karen found a tourist map in a brochure rack and we oriented ourselves in the town. I got up to pay for our snack. That's when I saw it: a yellowed newspaper clipping Scotch-taped to the wall. At first there was nothing startling about it. It was a picture of a successful angler, a grinning fisherman who might been photographed with a walleye in Wisconsin or a bonefish in Key West.

But this fisherman was astride an organism rent from the Jurassic. It appeared enormous and ancient. Pointed snout. Gaping gills. Pointed, bony plates running its length. Huge toothless mouth open in the thin air. The thing was so big the photographer could only squeeze the creature's head in the frame. It struck me as spooky. It was a Columbia River white sturgeon.

◈

ACTUALLY, to call a sturgeon a dinosaur is an understatement. The white sturgeon species dates back to the Cretaceous—the same era as *Triceratops*. Sturgeon as a group took shape some 250 million years ago and have gone through small, cosmetic changes since. (For reference, we modern *Homo sapiens* are around 100,000 years old.) Sturgeon swam Planet Earth when the seven modern continents were merged in one supercontinent, Pangea. In those days, the Appalachians were as high as the Himalayas are now and the Himalayas didn't exist. Sturgeon are older than North America. They predate the Atlantic Ocean.

Sturgeon are bottom-feeders, in the best sense of the word. Think of a shop vac with fins. Their long, spade-shaped snout is angled to rummage through sediment, turning up clams, crawfish, anchovies, dead fish, and other morsels. Barbels—long mustaches of tissue—drip on either side of the mouth, equipped with thousands of chemical receptors so the fish can sample the river detritus before actually putting it in its mouth. The fish have other receptors—basically external taste buds—all over their snouts. They can detect parts per billion, sifting through the muck at the bottom of the river for tasty morsels. The mouth is a long tube that stretches like a fleshy hose. On an adult, the mouth's diameter is sufficient to inhale a soccer ball.

The sturgeon's eyes are large but dim, reminding me of the eyes of a pig. Sturgeon do not swim as much as lurk, hanging slow and suspended in the depths. The body is thickest just behind the head, then tapers into a narrow isthmus before flaring into the tail. The tail is tall and sweeping, like that of a thresher shark. The dorsal fin is low and slanted and perched toward the rear like the fin on a '57 Chevy. Sturgeon are hard to the touch, almost as if covered with a shell. Like the skin of a shark, their epidermis has a sandpaper quality. A serrated ridge runs down the dorsal line and each outer edge. On young fish, these bony plates (called scutes) are so sharp they can cut your hand. They deter shark teeth, spear points, or the weapons of other predators.

But to describe a white sturgeon one must emphasize this fact: They are big. An adult sturgeon is large enough to saddle. Females are larger than males. The largest, scientifically valid specimen was captured in Canada's Fraser River in 1897 and weighed 1,387 pounds. However, fish up to 1,800 pounds (as much as a bison bull) have been reported, although not reliably weighed. White sturgeon grow fifteen feet long, which is longer than any car I have ever owned. White sturgeon are the largest freshwater fish in North America. By far. It takes time to reach such mass. When one cuts a sturgeon's scute in half, the interior reveals annual rings not unlike the rings of a tree trunk. With a microscope, one can count these rings. The trouble is that the rings tend to blur after one hundred years, so they may live longer. They are among the longest-lived fishes on Earth. White sturgeon, like chinook or king or sockeye salmon, are anadromous. That is, they are creatures of both ocean and river.

LEWIS AND CLARK arrived thirteen years too late to name the Columbia River. That river was named by American navigator Robert Gray for his ship, *Columbia Reviva,* and indirectly after that other explorer, Christopher Columbus.

Lewiston, Idaho, and Clarkston, Washington, straddle the

Snake River, and by all rights, the Snake was to have been named for Lewis. When the expedition was done and Clark mapped their journey, he labeled the Columbia's big, enigmatic tributary the Lewis River. That name stuck for decades.

That was the deal: Explore the country, name a river. The bigger the expedition, the larger a river. The Canadian explorers have their rivers: Simon Fraser; Alexander MacKenzie. Rivers named for Escalante and Gunnison drain the American Southwest. William Clark has a fork of the Columbia and a fork of the Yellowstone named in his honor. The Snake, Clark assumed, would be named for Lewis. The name might have stuck, had Lewis's life not ended in the scandal of suspected suicide and poor bookkeeping.

But what a river! A mighty torrent, pouring out of the jagged shadow of the Grand Tetons, rushing out of the mountains and across the Great Basin desert, sweeping a wide arc through southern Idaho, slicing basaltic layers of Hells Canyon, the deepest gorge in the United States, and tumbling some one thousand raucous miles before giving rise to the Columbia in southeastern Washington.

But it was not to be. The Snake is the Snake. The river is not named for any reptile. *Snake* is a label that Europeans placed on a tribe of Indians. These Indians are no longer called the Snake Indians by the whites, and they never were called the Snake Indians by themselves or other Indians. So as a name, Snake signifies nothing. A couple of rivers are named after Meriwether Lewis. One is the Lewis River in northwestern Wyoming, flowing out of Yellowstone National Park, Lewis never came within one hundred miles of this modest rivulet. There is also the Lewis River flowing south out of the Cascade mountains of Washington state. And near Astoria is the Lewis and Clark River, which flows into the Columbia right behind Fort Clatsop. But those rivers are not the Snake. Not by a long shot.

Perhaps that is the greatest prize of those lucky few born to be explorers: a name sprawled across a map. The land marked for posterity. For eternity? Well, no. Not eternity. No one gets eternity. Except possibly the sturgeon.

KAREN AND I wanted to see sturgeon. We were driving down the Snake River Canyon, toward the Columbia River. On Highway 12 outside Clarkston, Washington, horses had escaped their pasture and slowed traffic. Driving up Alpowa Canyon in southeastern Washington, the land smelled of dust and sage. Clumps of tumbleweed somersaulted across the highway like herds of skeletal deer. One bounced off the bumper, swept the hood and windshield, and lodged under the canoe.

But on the plateau beyond Alpowa Canyon and the Touchet River, the highway crossed the irrigated farmland of south central Washington. Trucks hauled potatoes, sweet corn, sugar beets, along with crates of pears and Washington's famous apples. We stopped at a fruit stand and bought four kinds of apples and two types of pears, all plump with Columbia and Snake River water, pumped from the rivers and sprinkled over the orchards. The fruit was so delicious we bought a couple more bags. We drove through vineyards that smelled exactly like the artificial flavoring in purple Kool-Aid. Only it was the smell of real grapes.

We passed quickly through the Tri-Cities of Kennewick, Pasco, and Richland, where the Snake River flows into the

Columbia. The Hanford Nuclear Reservation is upstream from here, the only free-flowing stretch of the Columbia in the United States. It's free of hydroelectric dams, but the land is so contaminated with radiation that even the tumbleweed is somewhat radioactive.

The Columbia stretched broadly across the desert. A wind blew upstream. We made camp at an island called Crow Butte State Park, where Lewis and Clark camped on their Columbia descent. We set up our stove to the lee side of the Subaru, so the wind wouldn't blow out the little flame. We watched the surface of the Columbia turn to whitecaps. Big river.

Lewis and Clark called the aboriginal people of this river the Chinook Indians. There is a word from the Chinook language that has survived into unabridged dictionaries and the lingo of the Pacific Northwest. The word is *skookum*. Skookum means *big* or *powerful*. In its original context, the word had a spiritual connotation. A grizzly or a king salmon is a *skookum* creature. I once asked a ranger from North Cascades National Park about the difficulty of a particular hike, and he replied, "It depends on how skookum you are."

Several locales in the Pacific Northwest are called *skookum-chuck*. In Chinook, *chuck* means *water*. So skookumchuck was a place of powerful water—a rapid or waterfall. In the Pacific Northwest, the Corps faced skookumchuck rapids daily. The river flexed its muscle in roiling, angry stretches of white water, thrusting hundreds of thousands of gallons downstream each second. Wherever the river was pinched or obstructed by basalt outcrops, the water pounded the rock, pulverizing itself against the basalt until the air filled with mist and noise. The rapids grew as the expedition continued downstream. The crude boats leaked, shipped water, capsized, and high-centered on rocks. The sodden hulls must have felt leaden under the paddle.

The men were eager to make the Pacific, so they took chances. They covered thirty miles daily. None had life jackets. Several members of the expedition did not know how to swim. But they ran whatever rapids they thought they could get away with. Sometimes they braved a dozen and more rapids a day. I imagined Toussaint Charbonneau, whom Clark described as "perhaps the most timid riverman in the world." Sacagawea and their infant son, Pomp, were in the canoe, helpless. Charbonneau must have been terrified. The Corps's courage must have approached fatalism. On the Columbia, the rapids had become waterfalls, and running them resembled suicide.

Celilo Falls dropped thirty-eight feet. Here the Indians had built elaborate scaffolds, where they stood over the raging falls to spear salmon in the autumn. This is one of the great icons of the Pacific Northwest: the power of the fish fighting the power of the river, with the daring and power of the man plucking the strong, healthy fish from the white water with a long-handled spear or net.

When the Corps came through, the river was at its autumn low. But the falls were still impassable. The men remained on shore and walked the boats downstream by handheld lines rather than run Celilo Falls. They portaged another twenty-foot drop at the mouth of the Deschutes River, lugging the boats overland.

At The Dalles, the entire force of the Columbia River was squeezed through a forty-five-foot gap of rock. The river formed a raging gutter of water and stone. The men considered portaging this appalling stretch of white water, but found the banks too steep and rocky to lug the boats over. Although the area of The Dalles has since been flooded by a dam, it is believed to have been a Class V rapid by today's river runners' standards. Such white water is virtually unrunnable, even by gutsy paddlers and modern equipment.

The captains divided the expedition into those who could swim and those who could not. The nonswimmers lugged the rifles, powder, and papers over the rocky ground. The swimmers braved The Dalles. (Truth be told, if the boaters capsized in such furious water, swimming would have done little good.) Indians lined the banks, waiting to witness the excitement of a wreck and the opportunity to salvage flotsam. One by one the boatmen shot through The Dalles. Soaked, but intact and upright. They continued downstream.

When Karen and I drove toward the city of The Dalles, Oregon, Celilo Falls was under thirty feet of reservoir water. Lewis and Clark had a difficult time getting canoes down this river. Today the dams, dredged channels, locks, and reservoirs allow oceangoing barges to haul freight some 465 miles upstream. Commercial shipping continues from Astoria, Oregon, to the inland ports of Clarkston and Lewiston.

All this came at a price. A price paid in fish. Today's salmon and steelhead runs are but a fragment of their former selves. But Karen and I saw aluminum-hull boats bobbing among the waves, fishing rods bowing to the current. Huge landing nets stood over the sterns like flags. Below The Dalles Dam there still stand a few scaffolds, where Native Americans wait days at a time to dip-net a salmon. Both fish and fishermen are survivors, fighting the odds.

At The Dalles we stopped at an auto parts store and bought new windshield wiper blades. Just then the sky opened up. Rain poured from the sky like the water was fleeing something in the heavens. Any traveler—in a dugout canoe or a Subaru wagon—

who travels down the Columbia Gorge cannot help but be struck by the changing landscape. At The Dalles, the land is desert, reminding one of the interior of Australia. Here the land receives fifteen inches of rain annually. But thirty miles downriver, the forest is cloaked in oak and pine and annual rainfall approaches thirty inches. Another thirty miles and the fir forest is moist and lush, soaked in seventy inches of rain annually.

As we drove on, I found Woody Guthrie's song in my head: *Roll on, Columbia, roll on / Your power is turning our darkness to dawn / Roll on, Columbia, roll on!*

That anthem of the Pacific Northwest was taught to my elementary school music class as a regional folk song. In fact, Woodie Guthrie's tune is federal propaganda. In the 1930s, Franklin Roosevelt was trying to dig the country out of the Great Depression. Among his make-work projects was an enormous, publicly owned hydroelectric system in the Northwest. Roosevelt faced steep political opposition from the big private utilities who stood to lose from such a proposition. The utilities hired movie stars to help sway public opinion against FDR. So Roosevelt hired a flat-broke folksinger named Woodrow Wilson Guthrie to travel, with a battered guitar and a government chauffeur, from the mouth of the Columbia to its source. Guthrie wrote twenty-six songs in as many days. The most famous of them stuck in my brain like a cocklebur in a sock.

In the end, FDR won his battle with the power companies. Over the coming decades the Columbia was harnessed in some fourteen major dams. There are another dozen on the Snake. The skookum energy of The Dalles and Celilo Falls were harnessed to spin turbines. The largest of the Columbia River dams is Grand Coulee, and behind that, the flaccid Columbia is known as

Franklin D. Roosevelt Lake. As I write this, power from the Columbia River hydroelectric grid powers my word processor.

The first of Roosevelt's federal dams was Bonneville Dam, which pinches shut a narrow piece of the Columbia just upstream from Portland, Oregon. Bonneville Dam is 150 miles upstream from the Pacific. If you were to ride a powerboat up the Columbia from Astoria, Oregon, the first thing to stop you would be Bonneville Dam. It is named for an Army captain, one Benjamin de Bonneville, an explorer who staked out the Oregon Trail. The dam, Karen and I were told, was a place to find sturgeon.

COLUMBIA RIVER SALMON—coho, king, and sockeye—are famous for their epic, tragic spawning runs. Geographers can define the Pacific Northwest by mapping the waters where salmon run. The spawning fish swim up the streams of the Coast Ranges, clear into the mountain lakes of central Idaho. Salmon hatch in the cold, rocky headwater brooks, wash downstream as smolts, mature in the ocean, then flash upstream again to spawn once and die. The fact that the fish find their way from the vast reaches of the Pacific back to their home waters is one of the great wonders of nature. Another is the fish making the unusual, painful transition from freshwater, to saline, to fresh again.

European Americans are inordinately fond of *salmonids*—spotted fish including trout, char, and salmon. They are tasty, to be sure, but part of their importance to our culture comes from the elite prejudices of seventeenth century anglers like Sir Izaak Walton and Charles Cotton. Because of such biases, I fear sturgeon do not get their due.

Sturgeon, too, are anadromous, swimming up freshwater streams from the ocean to spawn. Historically, uncounted thousands of spawning-age sturgeon—fish ten and fifteen feet long—swam up the Columbia, over Celilo Falls, and into the Snake and Salmon Rivers of Idaho and the Columbia of central Washington, even into British Columbia. Unlike salmon, sturgeon can pass between freshwater and saltwater with relative ease. They can remain in the river for decades or forgo the ocean altogether.

Sturgeon will also run up one river one year, return to the ocean, and swim up another river another year. In 1980 the Mount St. Helens eruption dumped millions of tons of ash into the Columbia River. Downstream, some white sturgeon temporarily abandoned the Columbia, pioneering new rivers. Sturgeon tagged in the Columbia River were recaptured in rivers hundreds of miles up and down the coast. Sturgeon, too, are explorers.

When dams were built on the Columbia, promises were made so that the salmon would still run. The promises proved empty. Great feats of engineering—fish ladders, barges, hatcheries—have rarely proven successful for salmon. But they failed the sturgeon altogether. The sturgeon were bottom-feeders, hardly worthy of consideration. And so the dams have cut the Columbia and Snake Rivers like a sharp hoe chops a water moccasin.

In the 150 miles of river between Bonneville Dam and the Pacific Ocean are perhaps a million sturgeon. Here the fish still have free run to the ocean.

The Columbia River reaches 1,100 miles above Bonneville Dam. Plus there are several hundred miles of sturgeon water on the Snake. This is all segmented by dams. Sturgeon are hemmed between curtains of concrete, isolated in small, fragmented populations that may or may not be large enough to sustain themselves in coming decades.

Upstream from Bonneville Dam, for more than 95 percent of the Columbia Basin, sturgeon fishing is catch-and-release, where it is allowed at all. The populations simply cannot spare the fish. White sturgeon in Idaho's Kootenai River are an official endangered subspecies because of dams on that tributary. (That's not unusual. Some two-thirds of the sturgeon populations in North America are threatened or endangered.)

But downstream from Bonneville Dam, the Columbia River white sturgeon appears to thrive, offering a glimpse of how the river used to be.

IN OCTOBER 1805, Lewis and Clark camped upstream of modern Portland. They noted that the river shore rose and fell over the course of the day. They were only a few feet above sea level and were witnessing the tides. The forested knob of basalt called Beacon Rock was the dominant landmark in that day. Now the gray wall of Bonneville Dam dominates this scene.

Today, thousands of travelers on Interstate 84 stop at Bonneville Dam. The dam itself is aging and the concrete is faded to a blotchy beige, but the picnic grounds are handsome and expensively groomed. Travelers rest here, pausing to walk through the interpretive displays in the dam. A few come to fish for sturgeon. To hunt dinosaur.

To hunt the dinosaur, it turns out, one needs a very big slingshot. No kidding. We pulled into the little parking lot at the foot of Bonneville Dam and there they were: slingshots ten feet long.

Sturgeon are often found at the foot of dams. Turbines stun and pulverize fish unlucky enough to be swept through them, sending a chum line downstream. This steady food supply can be a great windfall for sturgeon. Sturgeon fishermen know this and concentrate their efforts in such promising locales.

At the foot of Bonneville Dam we found Stan and Mary Southworth, of Port Hadlock, Washington, arming their giant slingshot. Stan and Mary had pitched a small camp under a blue tarp on the lee side of their pickup. A pot of tea water steamed on a propane stove. There was a small cooler with lunch, and much larger ones for fish. Stan wore a T-shirt with a sturgeon on the front, like a groupie advertising his favorite rock band. On his belt he wore a carpenter's tape. The tape was important: He was only allowed to keep fish between forty-two and sixty inches in length. Anglers were required to throw back the little ones and also to release the larger brood stock.

Stan's rod was a beefy, fourteen-foot surf-casting model. The hook was as long as a finger and baited with a piece of fish. The line was twenty-five-pound test, although with careful work Stan has landed fish weighing several hundred pounds on the outfit. But it was not the rod that caught my eye. It was the slingshot.

THE SLINGSHOT was propped up on a steel frame, aimed over the river. The Y was perhaps four feet across. The bands were inch-thick tubes of rubber with a leather pouch. Next to the slingshot was a five-gallon plastic bucket on a stand. Stan pulled line off the rod, spooling it around the bucket. At the end of the line, near the hook, was a twelve-ounce sinker—a piece of lead the size of a small pear.

Stan put the sinker into the pouch of the slingshot. He then hooked the pouch to a boat winch, the kind cranked by hand. "You might want to step back," Stan said, turning the crank and stretching the rubber bands tighter and tighter. "Just in case."

As ingenious as the weapon was, it appeared very homemade and threatened to fly apart at any minute, sending the hook and lead wickedly in some untoward direction. Everyone stepped away from the contraption. I took cover behind Stan's pickup, peeking around the corner.

Stan turned the crank. The slingshot grew tense. The rubber bands stretched and stretched until the rubber wouldn't stretch any more. The straining outfit trembled and quivered with kinetic energy. Stan gave me a smile.

"Ready?"

I nodded.

Stan slapped the lever on the winch and—*thwap*—the line catapulted into the sky. Spools of line whirled off the plastic bucket faster than one could watch. The launched weight took the trajectory of a well-driven golf ball. We visored out the sun with our hands as the parabola of line flew. It landed with such force that Stan tightened his grip on the rod so it wouldn't be yanked from his hands. The sinker plunked far into the river.

"How far did it go?" I asked.

"Oh," Stan said, "maybe three hundred."

"Yards? Three hundred yards?"

"Yeah. Maybe a little farther."

That's how you cast for sturgeon.

Stan inserted the rod handle in a large wooden block with

holes bored for that purpose. The rod tip pointed skyward. Then he walked down the lot to where the other fishermen were bull-shitting and smoking cigarettes. We waited.

OUT IN THE RIVER, sturgeon leaped like sky-hopping whales. As they jumped, their pale bellies flashed in the sun. Sturgeon are creatures of the deep waters, sometimes dwelling several hundred feet down on the bottom of the ocean. They do not feed on aerial insects. Yet here they were, leaping like rainbow trout doing water ballet. Nobody knows why they do this.

"Maybe they just enjoy it," Stan said. "I think they just like to catch air."

The tales of sturgeon fishermen outdo the usual fishing yarns because with sturgeon, there is no need to exaggerate. Like the old joke about the Texan who caught fish so big he measured them between the eyes. With a sturgeon, you could do that. No problem.

All sturgeon anglers I spoke to agreed that a hooked adult sturgeon can pull a boat upstream against the current of the Columbia. I doubted this, since none of these anglers seemed to own a boat. But a researcher I interviewed said he hooked a Snake River sturgeon while his boat was anchored on shore. The fish, he said, so strained the boat's bow line that it uprooted a sagebrush to which the boat was tied, before taking the boat upstream.

Some of the most colorful tales come from the era when fishing for sturgeon was a major business along these rivers. The roe of sturgeon is caviar and has long been valuable. Pioneers also caught sturgeon for meat, salting the flesh in barrels. Traditionally they caught them with trotlines—ropes or cables fixed to shore, baited with a hook, and left midstream for days. When a fish straightened a line, the angler would hook a team of draft horses to the line and pull the fish ashore. A large sturgeon can outweigh a horse, and there are legends about sturgeon pulling horses to watery deaths. I could not verify these stories, but I talked to otherwise skeptical scientists who believe them. When tractors became affordable, they replaced the horses. Cables can be seen today, ingrown in the bases of trees on the shores of Northwest rivers, where trotlines were grounded in decades past. Sturgeon now rarely reach the enormous sizes of the past. The fish don't live as long and do not have as much food. But they are big enough for these anglers, waiting for a bite at the tailwater of Bonneville Dam.

As Stan waited for a fish to claim his bait, Karen and I walked the grounds of Bonneville Dam. We started at the visitor center, a kind of propaganda clearinghouse for the Corps of Engineers. An elevator took us into the bowels of the dam, where visitors watched the fish ladder. Families stood before the laminated glass windows that glowed green like large-screen televisions. The water flowed past at seven miles per hour. Glistening, muscular coho salmon and steelhead trout occasionally wiggled past a window, flashing like slabs of living silver. The numbers of salmon have dropped alarmingly in recent years and there is real doubt that they will survive in decades to come. This added a bitter sadness to an otherwise joyous spectacle.

Sturgeon rarely use fish ladders and we did not expect to find them here. But as I watched for salmon, I noticed a peculiar shadow in the bottom of the window. At first I thought I imagined it, since I had sturgeon on my mind. I stared into the water, and in a minute it materialized again. A dark giant of a fish. It dwarfed even the largest steelhead to pass the window, seeming even larger since we could see only a portion of it in the limits of the window.

The shape faded into the watery gloom, then materialized again, never clear, but at moments unmistakable. Where the salmon struggled and churned their way upstream, this sturgeon waited placidly at the bottom of the concrete trough, exhibiting the patience learned over a couple hundred million years. It was impossible to tell if the sturgeon was heading upstream, following some timeless instinct to fight the current and spawn, or whether the fish was being washed down from the pool above.

WHEN WE RETURNED to the anglers at the base of Bonneville Dam, Stan's rod still pointed skyward. Mary gave us a sample of smoked sturgeon caught the previous season. We ate it and complimented them on it. We spoke of fish and fish politics. Of how the Columbia River was once the most productive salmon stream in the world, supporting people over tens of thousands of years. And how the dams threaten to end all that in less than a century. How it will be a hell of a battle to get even a portion of that back, if it is possible at all.

Then all conversation stopped. Stan's rod bowed, and he scooped it out of its holder.

Compared to the fun of firing the slingshot, landing the fish seemed anticlimactic. Stan didn't need a draft horse to tow in this fish, but it still fought in ardent protest. Stan muscled the rod up and down, taking in slack with the reel every time he pulled the rod back. After twenty minutes, a long, white fish flashed near shore.

The anglers' parking lot was perhaps one hundred feet above the river, separated by a boulder riprap. Another angler clambered down the rocks to land the fish as Stan kept the line tight. The volunteer knelt beside the fish, stretched a carpenter's tape, and shouted back the measurement. Fifty-two inches made it a legal catch. Stan thought it over. Anglers are allowed to keep only ten sturgeon annually, and he is choosy.

"Okay," he said. "I'll keep it."

Stan clambered down the rocks to kill the fish and hauled it back up the embankment. At the parking lot, he spent an hour peeling the sandpaper skin off the fish and cutting off the fillets. He dulled three knives in the process. He showed us the fish's notochord. Sturgeon have no bones—no real spine. The "skeleton" is cartilage, like that of a shark. Stan was painstaking with his knife, separating the edible from the inedible.

"I figure if the fish is giving his life for my dinner table, the least I can do is not waste any of it," he said. The resulting fillets were as long as his leg.

Sturgeon remains an important commercial and sport fish in the reach of water between Bonneville Dam and the Pacific. The commercial fishery has grown as salmon have dwindled. Karen and I found sturgeon for twelve dollars a pound at a gourmet grocery in Portland—a higher price than salmon.

As Stan butchered his catch, the gray wall of Bonneville Dam rose behind him. Power-line towers—painted in bands of orange and white—rose above that. Electricity hummed and snapped in the suspended wires. We barter with the river, try to turn it to our advantage, hoping what we gain is worth the price. A froth of oxygenated water bubbled from the churning turbines of the dam named for Captain Bonneville. Far upstream, water continued to collect in the huge slackwater lake named for President Roosevelt.

Captain Lewis, I'm sorry your name was not given permanently to the great tributary of the Columbia. But pay no mind. This is all fleeting. All maps fade. These names will be forgotten. These dams will crumble. Only the rivers remain. And older than that, the sturgeon.

Chapter 11

Downriver

GREAT PLAINS
COTTONWOOD
Populus deltoides occidentalis

THIRTY-FIRST BIRTHDAYS COME BUT ONCE A LIFETIME. Thank God. It was my thirty-first, the last day of September. Autumn rode in at full gallop. My mood sunk cold and dark as obsidian. I had no excuse for ill spirits. We were in Fort Benton, Montana, an idyllic wheat ranching town on the Missouri River. After agriculture, a secondary component of Fort Benton's economy is tourism, particularly tourism inspired by the Lewis and Clark Expedition. Renovated historic storefronts line the town's river frontage. But in autumn, the ice cream shops and museums were boarded closed. Stately cottonwood trees towered over the riverfront walkway, bending and rustling to a stout upriver wind.

Karen and I visited a memorial to Fort Benton's most storied citizen, a sheepdog named Shep. Back in the 1930s, a local sheepherder died and his coffin was sent by train for burial back East. Shep watched the boxcar door roll shut on his master's casket and was left behind. After that, the dog greeted every train that visited the station, awaiting his master's return. For years. The dog's loyalty attracted sentimental newsmen from across the country. Shep could not have received more ink had the dog hired a press agent.

I could not make up my mind about Shep. Why did we admire him so? Did he represent eternal faith and hope? Or was he simply nostalgic, wasting his time longing for a past that could never return?

Eventually the dog grew deaf and stiff. Shep stepped in front of a train and got squashed. Now, Shep is immortalized in bronze. Down the block is another statue, this one of Lewis, Clark, Sacagawea, and little Pomp. As Karen and I walked the deserted riverfront, the wind blew so strong it almost ruffled the hair on the statues. I turned up my collar and shrugged out the chill.

Thirty-first birthdays send the mind probing within. And the mind does not always like what it finds. Take Capt. Meriwether Lewis, who celebrated his thirty-first on August 18, 1805, up past the headwaters of the Missouri. He wrote:

"I reflected that I had as yet done but little, very little, indeed, to further the hapiness of the human race. . . . I viewed with regret the many hours I have spent indolence . . . But since they are past and cannot be recalled, I dash the gloomy thought and resolved in future . . . to live for mankind as I have heretofore lived for myself."

Damn, Meriwether. Sounds like a hatchling midlife crisis to me. For someone with a heroic reputation, Lewis was a tortured figure. Upon returning home, he was dogged by allegations of financial misconduct and perhaps manic depression and alcoholism as well. The expedition's books were a mess. Lewis had told Congress the trek would cost $2,500, but he ran up bills totaling nearly $39,000. Lewis was on his way to Congress to explain the expedition's finances when he died of a mysterious gunshot wound at a backwoods inn in Tennessee. Although some historians hold that Lewis was murdered, Lewis probably fired the fatal bullet through his own chest. A good shrink and a Prozac prescription might have saved his life.

Dash those gloomy thoughts, Meriwether. Give yourself a break. Indolence is not so bad. Not compared with suicide.

So I dashed the gloomy thoughts myself, pledging heretofore to take life seriously, but not too seriously. After all, what better place to celebrate a birthday, celebrate life, than on a wild river? Like any good backtrack, our route had looped back on itself. Karen and I arrived at Fort Benton to canoe once again down the Upper Missouri. We were heading back down the Missouri, just as the Corps returned downriver in 1806. They were triumphant and homeward bound, coasting on the downstream current.

What brought Karen and me back? Paying customers, for one. We were joined by a dozen students on this trip. Karen was teaching photography, while our professor friend Lex Blood was lecturing on geology. We planned to paddle the "lover-to-lover" route. That is, from the mouth of the Marias River fifty miles down the Missouri to the Judith River. Lewis named the Marias after his heartthrob, while Clark named the Judith for the girl who would become his wife.

In summer at Fort Benton, guide services shuttle a steady flow of canoe-bound tourists up and down this segment of the Missouri. Fleets of canoes are a common sight. But in October, we figured we wouldn't see another soul for the next four days. The reason is simple: October is a gamble. Once on the river, you are committed for fifty miles. Arctic winds sometimes howl up this river, stopping canoes cold. Snow, even a blizzard, was quite possible. The weatherman had been cagey, not making any promises. But the Missouri, after all, is worth a gamble.

The Missouri is the nation's longest river, but a mere 149 miles of it is a federally protected Wild and Scenic River. It is a splendid place for a canoe trip, but this segment fails to capture the entire story of the river. The Missouri flows through seven states, impounded, diked, and leveed nearly all the way. Today's river is a third as wide as its original riverbed. By straightening curves, we have reduced the river's length by 120 miles. Because of our tinkering, the Missouri has lost 90 percent of its islands and sandbars, crucial habitat for a host of species. The Missouri is less and less a river and more and more a ditch. If I wanted to report on the reality of the Missouri, I should not indulge in another float here. I should visit the industrial riverfront of Great Falls. I should pick up trash along the Missouri in Kansas City or have water samples tested downstream from Omaha. But that would be too difficult. Too complicated. Too disheartening.

Dash these gloomy thoughts. Time to put on the river. Let the river work its magic.

EARLY THE NEXT MORNING, we drove to a bluff overlooking the confluence of the Marias and Missouri Rivers. Lewis and Clark climbed this bluff together during the upstream journey in May 1805, trying to figure out a riddle. Specifically, whether to follow the Marias or the Missouri.

In other seasons, in other places, the explorers would name rivers for presidents and for secretaries of state, war, and treasury: Jefferson, Madison, Smith, Dearborn, Gallatin. Or for lofty ideals: Wisdom and Philanthropy. But the captains were here in spring. The rivers were particularly lovely. Romance was on their minds. Lewis named the Marias River after Maria Wood, a young beauty who had captured his heart in Virginia. His journal gushes:

"It is true the hue of this troubled and turbulent stream but illy comport with the pure celestial virtues and amiable qualifications of that lovely fair one. But on the other hand it is a noble river . . . which passes through a rich, fertile and one of the most beautifully picturesque countries that I ever beheld."

Flattery got Lewis nowhere. Back home, Maria Wood rejected the hero captain. Some historians suspect that this heartbreak helped push Lewis over the edge. But today a disproportionate number of baby girls born in Montana are named Maria.

Our little caravan continued to Virgelle, a ferry town that is a ghost of itself since bridges have rendered ferries largely obsolete. Down to the water we toted our fleet: a homemade dory, three sea kayaks, and three canoes. We loaded each with sleeping bags, ice chests, wine bottles, propane stoves. Clothes squeezed in water-proof bags. Sloshing jugs of drinking water.

Freeboard disappeared under our cargo. As we packed, we chuckled smug, modern chuckles about the Lewis and Clark Expedition and the amount of *stuff* they brought along. How unlike the free-roaming Blackfeet and Crow nomads native to this land! The Corps towed a boat the size of a small recreational vehicle upstream from St. Louis. They packed a portable blacksmith shop, writing desks, an arsenal of weaponry including a small cannon. Buckskin, not nylon! Cast iron, not aluminum!

I figured each member of our party had about one hundred pounds of gear and supplies. We were camping four days. That's easy: twenty-five pounds of stuff per person per day. Meanwhile, the Corps left St. Louis with about thirty *tons* of gear. Roughly a ton of gear per member of the expedition who made it to the Pacific. But the Corps was gone more than two *years.* So each member of the expedition had roughly two pounds of equipment per day afield. By that measure, *they* were traveling light. Not us.

We pushed off. Even laden deep, the boats floated easily down the deep green water. I plunged a paddle into the water and saw its tip about three feet underwater. For the Missouri, this was quite clear. The river was at its autumn low. The current pulled us at about three miles per hour. The mosquitoes that plague the summer Missouri were dead, dead, dead. God rest their bloodthirsty souls. However, the brisk headwind still blew. The gusts impeded our progress, making us work for purchase against it.

The sandstone cliffs rose from the river, pockmarked with burrows of the bank swallows and gourd-shaped mud nests of cliff swallows. The nests were empty, summer birds unwilling to chance the weather. Still present were the hearty kingfisher and the cackle of a distant pheasant. Omnipresent pigeons flapped from the cliff, as content there as on a city viaduct. Flights of Canada geese rose from the distant grainfields. We heard their chuckling and then looked up to see migratory Vs take shape against the sky.

After the morning on the water, our legs cramped in the confines of the boats. We beached near the mouth of Little Sandy Creek, a trickling, saline affair that was hardly a creek at all. Karen lead the class up the bluff, discussing f-stops and meter readings and looking for a photogenic landscape. No problem finding one. The problem was trying to edit this sweeping drama into a 35-millimeter frame. An impossible chore, but not an unpleasant one. Wind rippled the river below us, the sun turning the water surface to diamonds. The photographers scattered across the slope, unaccustomed to so much space. I noticed the lenses turn toward the one kind of tree that grows here, lining the river as if planted in a row by an English gardener. Cottonwoods.

Farther downstream, at Eagle Creek, we again pulled ashore and pitched tents under another stand of cottonwoods. These trees, I realized, had been our constant companions as Karen and I retraced the Lewis and Clark adventures. The black cottonwood species along the Columbia. The narrowleaf, along the Yellowstone. These plains cottonwoods along the Missouri. The crisping leaves gave a leathery rattle. We collected dead branches and fibrous bark from the ground and built a fire against the dark and its inevitable companion, cold. The smoke wafted sweet and curled around us, infiltrating the fibers of our clothes and the roots of our hair. Cottonwood smoke smells like no other. We were hungry and we ate the most delicious stew ever concocted. We stared at the fire as if it were some Neolithic television. We fed the coals, laughing and talking until the embers glowed. Taking energy from cottonwood.

◆

THERE IS A JOKE among botanists: "Endangered plants are the little things you step on while searching for endangered animals."

Perhaps it is natural for humans, as animals, to focus on our fellow animals. But Meriwether Lewis was not bound by this convention. Lewis's mother was an herb doctor and wild-crafter who taught her son to be an expert and enthusiastic botanist. He collected plants under the most trying circumstances. On the return trip, in North Dakota, Lewis was shot in the butt in a hunting accident. He wrote one of his last journal entries while wounded, in pain, face-down in the bottom of a canoe. The entry was a description of a variety of cherry. He described the leaf in minute detail.

Lewis noted practical uses of the plants he found, including medicinal properties professed by local tribes. He wrote that some tribes said the glacier lily prevents pregnancy. (Don't try this one at home, boys and girls.) He also wrote that a daisy-like prairie blossom, the purple coneflower, was highly prized by the plains Indians for its power to treat snake bite. Today, this plant, *Echinacea,* is the most commonly used herb in alternative medicine, said to boost the immune system and fight the common cold.

The Corps of Discovery—almost entirely by the work of Lewis—collected, pressed, and described some 178 varieties of plants. Lewis used his full vocabulary of botanical jargon. The Montana state flower, the bitterroot, and the Idaho state flower, syringa, both credit Lewis in their scientific names, as does *Linum lewisii,* Lewis's flax. Ironic, since Lewis avoided Latin. Not only are several plant species named after Lewis, but so is the genus of the bitterroot. The diminutive flower known as the ragged robin is also known by its technical name, *Clarkia*. Lewis and Clark are credited with discovering three types of cottonwood tree: the black cottonwood, *Populus trichocarpa*, of the Columbia Basin; the narrowleaf cottonwood, *Populus angustifolia*, of the nation's interior; and *Populus deltoides occidentalis*, the Great Plains cottonwood.

In these arid grasslands, the cottonwood is quite often the only tree in sight, hugging the river like a child hugging its mother's skirt. A few yards beyond the river and the land stretches out in an infinity of bunchgrass and sagebrush. But along the river stand the trees. The cottonwood is entirely indebted to the river and never ventures far from it. For homesick wanderers from the oak-and-sycamore hills of Virginia and Kentucky, each cottonwood stand was a deciduous oasis.

"These appearances were quite reviving after the drairy country through which we were passing," Lewis wrote. The Corps not only described the cottonwood, but exploited it. Cottonwood provided shade on hot days and campfire fuel on cold evenings. When chased by grizzlies, the explorers ascended cottonwood trees.

But the utility of cottonwoods shone in June 1805, during the monthlong portage around Great Falls. The Corps faced the daunting task of toting tons of boats and gear some twenty-five miles around the cascades. Their fleet included a steel boat frame that Lewis had had built in West Virginia. The plan was to cover the frame with elk skins, seal the seams with pine tar, and have a tough, portable boat when the going got tough. The men had dubbed the craft the *Experiment*, and had already hauled it a couple thousand miles upstream. But now they had to get the *Experiment* and their other boats around the Great Falls.

At the foot of the falls stood a single cottonwood tree. It was about two feet in diameter, the only substantial specimen for twenty miles. Six men chopped the tree down, then sawed the trunk into slices. The slices were wheels. They removed the mast from a pirogue to make axles. They perched a boat on this rickety contraption. With the scrap lumber, they built two more carts. They pushed these wagons across the plains, even erecting a sail to exploit the prairie wind, sailing on dry land.

The portage was tortuous. The weather alternated between blazing heat, hailstorms, and cloudbursts that filled dry washes with flash floods. Mosquitoes swarmed. Cacti punctured their feet. The men worked until they could not stand. The cottonwood proved brittle and the carts broke under the weight, forcing difficult repairs.

Over a month of toil, the men shuttled the boats and gear beyond the falls. The men killed elk and bison for skins to cover Lewis's steel boat frame. Elk and bison were everywhere, but trees were scarce. There were no pines to provide tar. Lewis tried to make do with tallow and beeswax. The untreated hides held together, but just barely.

Eventually, the time came to see if the *Experiment* would float. It did. For a while. But gradually, water seeped in, swamping the boat and sending it to the bottom of the river. The *Experiment* was a miserable failure. All the work and expense was for naught.

Lewis was mortified. Clark was thinking ahead. Perhaps privately predicting the failure of Lewis's experiment, Clark had sent scouts to look for trees. Several miles upstream, the men found two cottonwoods, one with a trunk twenty-five feet long, another thirty-three feet long, and each three feet across. Within five days, the men had the trees hollowed into dugout canoes. The expedition could continue upstream, paddling toward the source of the Missouri. Cottonwoods saved the day.

As historian Paul Cutright put it: "Of all western trees [the cottonwood] contributed more to the success of the Expedition than any other. . . . Though we think it probable that they would have successfully crossed the continent without the cottonwood, don't ask us how!"

AT EAGLE CREEK, we camped under a generous canopy of cottonwoods. The wind picked up past midnight. Brittle dead branches creaked in the wind over our heads. Old cottonwoods die from the top down, occasionally sending limbs and segments of trunks crashing to the ground. In the dead of night, Karen and I picked up the tent and moved beyond the reach of widowmakers. Throughout the night, the autumn wind bellowed our tent, as if to turn it inside out. We caught our sleep in little snatches.

At dawn the wind whipped dust off the grasslands and foamed the river into whitecaps. The wind blew headlong upstream. We were going to have to paddle against it. Overhead, battalions of clouds amassed for an assault. Lex pulled me and Karen aside. "We could be in for a long day," he said. "I think we better get the boats on the river as soon as we can."

We ate a hurried breakfast, turning our backs to the wind to keep airborne grit off our plates. The aluminum lid blew off the oatmeal pot and Nick raced it to the river. After breaking camp, we lashed the gear into our boats. We bundled up and shoved off. I zipped my life jacket snug, pulled my cap tight, and paddled hard to make progress against the wind.

For safety's sake, our fleet clustered in a tight bunch. Whitecaps rocked the boats, water splashing over the bows. We rounded the first bend in the river, fighting the wind all the way. There was a beautiful power in this cold breeze. Like autumn itself, the wind was bracing. Invigorating. Vigor—from the Latin word for *lively*—for *life*. My face stung, blood rushing to the surface.

This went on for a couple hours. But the wind did not last. At first it lapsed only briefly. Then the choppy water went slack. "I think it may have blown itself out," Karen said. I was dubious, but an hour passed without wind. My grip relaxed on the paddle.

"There's a lesson in that," Lex said. "Sometimes, in spite of all the evidence to the contrary, things are not as bad as they appear."

KAREN AND I learned of the Great Plains cottonwood from Susan Lenard. We met Susan the previous July in Helena, Montana. Susan is an intense young woman with straight brown hair braided in the back of her head. She has a runner's build and metabolism.

Susan Lenard is such an enthusiastic birder that she takes an expensive pair of Austrian binoculars even on short strolls. This passion led to her employment with the Montana Audubon Society. The Audubon Society is a group that has fought on behalf of birds since the days when the women's hat industry was their largest threat. Today the Montana chapter of the society is focusing on conserving cottonwood trees.

Lewis noted the bird life amid the Missouri's cottonwoods: "Innumerable litle birds . . . sung most inchantingly; I observe among them the brown thrush, Robbin, turtle dove, linnit goaldfinch, the large and small blackbird wren and several others. . . ."

Susan said 60 percent of the birds that breed in the West breed in the riverside zones dominated by cottonwoods, even though that habitat makes up a small fraction of the total landscape. One-third of Montana bird species nest in cottonwoods. They range from bald eagles and Canada geese, weaving ragged platforms of sticks in the treetops, to thumb-size chickadees and elfin little owls that nest in cavities in the trunks.

"It's not just birds," Susan said. "Elk and deer use cottonwoods for shelter during winter and to hide their young during the calving season. Beavers absolutely depend on them. Even fish use them: The trees provide shade, which helps keep the water cool enough to support trout. The trees' spreading root systems help prevent erosion."

The fact that any tree can grow in this arid land of poor soils is remarkable. Paradoxically, Great Plains cottonwoods grow in an arid land but are inefficient users of water. That is why they are never more than a stone's throw from the river.

Leaves, you may recall from biology class, extract carbon dioxide from the air, drawing this gas through pores called *stomata*. Inside the leaf, solar energy and carbon dioxide mix with water drawn from the tree's roots and trunk. The alchemy within the leaf creates oxygen, which is expelled, and sugar, which is consumed by the tree. Most plants simply shut down those stomata when they have taken in enough carbon dioxide to provide for their growth. But cottonwoods must make up for the poor soil in which they grow. So they leave those pores wide open, taking in carbon dioxide all day long. All that photosynthesis comes at a price to be paid in water. Because the Great Plains are so dry, cottonwoods can only live adjacent to reliable sources of water.

Cottonwoods earn their names each spring, when a mature tree may put forth 25 million tiny seeds, surrounded in fluffy, white "cotton." A favorable wind can blow the seeds a mile or more. If the seed lands on the river, the fluff keeps it afloat as it drifts downstream. On summer days, the cotton creates the illusion of a warm-weather blizzard.

A fortunate few seeds alight on riverbanks, islands, or freshly scoured gravel bars and germinate. Roots grow half a centimeter a day. The young trees are durable under flood, but doomed in drought. The seedling will grow into a mature cottonwood in 10 years. A tree may live 150 years, sheltering elk, warblers, and beer-swilling canoeists.

That is how it is supposed to work. That is how it has worked for thousands of years. Only now, there is a problem.

"Actually," Susan told us, "there are five major problems."

Thousands of dams, large and small, along with dikes and riprap, have changed river courses. No longer do the seasonal floods give cottonwoods the growing conditions they need. Where saplings do take root, they are often chewed down by cattle. In addition, cottonwoods must compete with exotic weeds, such as Russian olive and tamarisk. Although cottonwood makes poor lumber, it is sometimes cut for throwaway products, like cardboard and shipping crates.

"That's the picture," Susan said.

"Any good news?" I asked.

"Well, yeah," she said. "Not long ago, ranchers and farmers used to systematically cut cottonwood, stand by stand. They thought the trees—through transpiration—were guzzling water that could go to irrigation or livestock. But after they had destroyed the cottonwoods, they noticed the streams suffered even more. Without the shade, the sun evaporated more water than the trees transpired.

"The trout the ranchers liked to catch on Sundays were gone, as was the shade where they ate lunch during the haying season. Without shelter from winter winds, cows didn't put on as much weight as they did before.

"So the ranchers and farmers figured out removing the cottonwood was more detrimental than leaving it. Aside from cutting for homesites or lumber, you don't see as much cutting anymore. Actually, the ranchers and farmers I work with, they are on the land every day. They understand what's going on. They're just not sure what they can do about it.

"Conserving cottonwoods is a tough issue to rally people around," Susan said. "Trees don't have the charisma of, say, wolves or grizzly bears."

LEWIS AND CLARK descended the Missouri for the last time in 1806. But America wasn't done with the Missouri. Not by a long shot.

The river became the main thoroughfare from the eastern United States into the northern Rockies and Great Plains. The first fur trappers marched upstream as Lewis and Clark returned home. Gold prospectors followed the fur boom, in turn followed by cattle barons. For most of a century, the Missouri was virtually the only way goods traveled in and out of the nation's interior.

Steamboats hauled the loot from the frontier to the cities, and moved trade goods from the cities out to the frontier. Paddlewheels fought the current wherever the river was deep enough to provide draft. The boilers were fueled with seasoned cottonwood. When fully loaded and heading upstream, a steamboat burned thirty cords of wood a day. A cord is a stack of wood four feet by four feet by eight feet. Thirty cords fill a small barn. Cottonwood smoke hung over the Missouri like a shroud.

Opportunists called woodhawks mowed down the cotton-wood trees, bucked and split the logs, and sold the wood as soon it was cured. The result was kind of a buffalo slaughter executed with crosscut saws. Stumps lined the riverbanks. For a while, any man with an ax could make a living. Then railroads tracks were stitched across the plains. Everyone—riverboat captains, wood-hawks, longshoremen—went out of business.

The cottonwood trees we passed were the progeny of the survivors from the steamboat days. As we paddled down the Missouri, I looked for a new generation of young trees. I saw handsome, grandfatherly trees, some eighty feet tall and four feet thick at the trunk. But they were brittle and uniformly aged. The Missouri River was like a city populated only by retirees. Fast-growing and resilient, cottonwoods can withstand a lot of abuse. They withstood the woodhawks and they withstand the cattle. But everything has a breaking point. Future paddlers on this river may not enjoy the shade of the cottonwood.

OUR FEARS came true. The wind brought in a wet cold front. We paddled aggressively all morning, as if we had hope of out-running it. That afternoon it rained straight down on our heads. But in our rain gear, paddling was still tolerable, even enjoyable. The water was smooth, dimpled by the raindrops. The rain, we all agreed, was better than the headwind.

We camped early and stretched a dining fly between the trunks of two cottonwoods. Lex built a big fire, while someone uncorked a jug of red. We heated a pot of soup as the sun set. The dining fly snapped and flapped like a sail rigging in the wind, but we were snug under it.

Someone started singing show tunes. One Broadway hit followed another. We melted down the lyrics from *South Pacific* and *Sound of Music* and reforged them to the story of the Corps of Discovery. The songs were mildly obscene and seemed uproariously funny at the time. We all sang and then laughed and then stared quietly into the fire while the coyotes sang and laughed back at us. The fat prairie moon rose behind a veil of clouds. The morning, we knew, would break clear.

THE NEXT DAY Jim, expedition paleontologist, stepped ashore to take a leak and found a cliff face loaded with fossils. He showed us a sample of clamshells pressed to stone. Seventy-five million years old, Lex said. We passed a lowslung gravel bar called Wolf Island, where Captain Clark had speared a wolf with his espontoon.

Around the bend at Arrow Creek, which is neither dammed nor grazed heavily, the cottonwoods stood in stark contrast to the main Missouri. Trees flourished along the banks of the tributary; not only grandfather trees, but middle-aged ones and thick undergrowth of youngsters.

A bald eagle flushed ahead of us, instantly recognizable with its heavy, tugging wing beats and glowing white head and tail. We had seen several golden eagles, but this was the first bald eagle on this trip. Lewis and Clark noted scads of bald eagles along the Missouri, along with white pelicans and passenger pigeons. In the 1960s, Lewis and Clark historian Paul Cutright noted that bald eagles were rare on the Missouri, lamenting that America's national bird was facing extinction. In the years since Cutright wrote that, Americans banned the pesticide that damaged the eagle's eggshells. Eagles rebounded and are no longer endangered. During some seasons, in some places, it is not unusual to see dozens of bald eagles gathered on the Missouri. Sometimes, in spite of all the evidence to the contrary, things are not as bad as they might seem.

Five mule deer bucks bounded up a slope in the bouncing, four-footed hop called *stotting.* The little herd looked like a band of bank robbers making their getaway aboard pogo sticks. Fleeing predators is a serious business, but so help me I can't see mule deer run without holding back a laugh.

OCTOBER IS MY FAVORITE MONTH. Except for nine or ten of the others. During October, October is my favorite. During October, I'm in love with October. Especially October days like our last one on the river. October smiled and the land and air were freshly washed and basked in sunlight, but touched with coolness. October lets you know she is the one calling the shots in this relationship. Remember that, she says, and we'll get along just fine.

On days like that, I would gladly pledge myself to October, promise to live my life faithfully with October only, forsaking all others. But October is fickle and always ends up leaving me. November blows in under the door and I wonder what I said to offend.

Winter was coming. Karen and I would soon be leaving the Lewis and Clark Trail, at least for a while. We wanted to camp on the Big Sur, hike in the Grand Canyon. We wanted to do more exploring. Then we would find a house-sitting gig for the winter. No road trip lasts forever. We would have to get serious, attending to the everlasting frontier called the future.

The Montana legislature had met and reinstalled a numeric speed limit. All across the state, road crews were erecting speed limit signs. Seemed everybody was eager to exhibit a little more common sense and be a little bit practical.

But not that day. That day it was me and October, holding hands, mooning at each other, wondering if there was a place where we could get a few minutes alone. Karen was in love, too. She kicked her feet up on the bow and stretched back over the gear in the canoe. She smiled at me, her face upside down. I looked at the paddle in my hands. Screw it, I thought, who needs to paddle on a day like this? What does a paddle do but hurry us down the river? Why not just keep floating? All the way to St. Louis. All the way to New Orleans.

A light breeze nudged us from behind. Neal and Pattie, in their tandem kayak, felt creative. Neal rifled through his duffel and extracted his long johns. They were a classic, red union suit, with the drop seat, long sleeves, and white buttons. Pattie ran the paddles up through the legs, then stretched the blades through the arms. She held this apparatus up, so the underwear formed a sail. The wind billowed the underwear-sail from behind and *voila!* the kayak coasted downstream and downwind, right past the rest of us. Sailing under the flag of Fruit of the Loom.

As their kayak sped downstream, it looked like a beet-red giant with a potbelly was levitating over the deck. Cows on shore saw it and fled with tails raised. Karen and I laughed. I thought benevolent thoughts about cows. God, I was in a good mood.

On the south shore, we passed a man and woman riding a pair of matched palominos on the short-grass bluffs. These were the first people outside our party we had seen since launching at Virgelle. They looked like they just rode off a photo shoot for a Marlboro cigarette ad. I waved and they doffed their Stetsons and waved them back.

For some reason, the riders brought to mind the 1955 movie about Lewis and Clark, *The Far Horizons.* It was a giant cheeseball of American cinema. Lewis was played by Fred MacMurray (later the father in *My Three Sons*) and Clark was portrayed by Charlton Heston (later president of the National Rifle Association). Donna Reed played Sacagawea in tight buckskin. In my mind, MacMurray and Heston saddled up alongside the Marlboro couple on the bank. They were the mythical West, as viewed from Hollywood and Madison Avenue. It's hogwash and we know it. But are any of us utterly divorced from the Western mythos? Not really. We love it. Part of us does, anyway. We want both versions—the real West and the romantic one. Or rather, we don't want either. We laugh off the kitsch of Fred MacMurray and Donna Reed. But if we are honest, we would also pass on the real Lewis and Clark Expedition. We would loathe the blizzards, the lice, the boils, the meals of dog meat and bison guts, the untreated disease and early deaths. The Hollywood Lewis and Clark bores us, but the real thing would likely kill us. Somewhere in between the two is the West we are looking for. It calls us out. It keeps us here.

Beyond the myth, the romance, and the hogwash, the other beings survive. They survive because of us or in spite of us. They do not flatter us with much concern. They exist on their own will. They are the grizzly and the coyote, the cutthroat trout and the cottonwood tree. Hope runs through their hearts. Hope enough for all of us.

My mood had brightened since my birthday. Rivers can do that. Where did that old pessimism come from, when the world is still this beautiful? Pessimism is a disease. Pessimism is the enemy. Pessimism did not ban DDT and save the bald eagle. It did not create Yellowstone National Park and protect the last few bison. It did not protect the grizzly bears of the Swan Range or the wolves and elk of the Rocky Mountains. Pessimism will not serve the prairie dog or the black-footed ferret. Pessimism did not help the sturgeon survive the countless ages, nor the little cutthroat trout survive in Griffin Creek. There is too much at stake for us to give pessimism a chance. There is still too much to be lost.

October whispered in my ear. "Never lose the joy," she said. "You lose the joy, and the weight of the world is going to squash you like a freight train."

We floated around the final bend, noting the bridge that marked the end of this journey. Beyond that, our shuttle van waited for us. To the south were rugged side canyons embroidered in pine and beyond that the low, long ridge of the Judith Mountains. Flowing from the south was the Judith River, cloaked in resplendent cottonwood. The mature trees were still a deep green, but the thick undergrowth trees—the young upstart saplings—were autumn gold, like some vibrant lining. The trees—yellow and green—were backlit in rich, autumn sun. The colors danced across my retinas.

Notes on Sources

Like many fans of American history and of American adventure, I am indebted to Stephen Ambrose's *Undaunted Courage* for repopularizing the Corps of Discovery. The Lewis and Clark journals have been edited several times and I depended on the abridged version by Bernard de Voto and the full journals by Gary E. Moulton. I would have floundered without two scholarly books on the expedition's biological discoveries—Paul Cutright's *Lewis and Clark: Pioneering Naturalists* and Raymond Burroughs's *Natural History of the Lewis and Clark Expedition.* The periodical *We Proceeded On,* published by the Lewis and Clark Trail Heritage Foundation, also proved invaluable.

I also depended on Silvio A. Bedinis's *Thomas Jefferson: Statesman of Science,* about the state of science in the United States during Jefferson's lifetime. *Buffalo Nation: History and Legend of the North American Bison,* by Valerius Geist, opened my mind about these stolid, solid creatures, as did the *Proceedings of the International Symposium on Bison Ecology and Management,* held at Montana State University in 1997 and edited by L. Irby and J. Knight. To learn about grizzly bears, one would do well to start with *The Great Bear Almanac,* by Gary Brown, and *Bear Attacks: Their Causes and Avoidance,* by Stephen Herrero.

Prairie Night: Black-Footed Ferrets and the Recovery of an Endangered Species, by Brian Miller, Richard Reading, and Steve Forrest, covers the intertwined fates of the black-footed ferret and the black-tailed prairie dog. *The Eastern Coyote: The Story of Its Success,* by Gerry Parker, details the expansion of the trickster east of the Mississippi. *Of Wolves and Men,* by Barry Lopez, and *Wildlife in America,* by Peter Matthiessen, both deserve status as natural history classics. On the subject of the westslope cutthroat trout, I relied on Patrick Trutter's *Cutthroat: Native Trout of the West.* To learn about whitebark pine, I read *Timberline: Mountain and Arctic Forest Frontiers,* by Stephen Arno and Ramona P. Hammerly, as well as the 1990 *Proceedings of the Symposium on Whitebark Pine Ecosystems,* sponsored by the U.S. Forest Service Intermountain Research Station and compiled by Wyman C. Schmidt Kathy J. McDonald.

A River Runs Through It and Other Stories, by Norman Maclean, along with the *American Authors Series: Norman Maclean,* edited by Ron McFarland and Hugh Nichols, offer insights about that great American author.

We also left ragged the *National Geographic's Field Guide to the Birds of North America,* the *Subaru Owners Manual,* and the *Montana State Fishing Regulations.*

Acknowledgments

Writing is often portrayed as an individual enterprise, but in fact is a team effort. It is impossible for me and Karen to thank everyone who helped us with this project, but unthinkable not to. I trust that the friends who let us sleep on their floors, camp in their yards, and dry wet gear in their garages will forgive us if we miss their names.

We thank people for their valuable professional time, including Raymond Rye, at the Smithsonian Institution; Michael Ober and staff at Flathead Valley Community College Library; Montana state biologists John Waller, Rick Mace, John Vore, John Fraley, and Dan Casey; Randy Matchett, Diane Boyd, and Joe Fontaine, of the U.S. Fish and Wildlife Service; Maria Mantis and Louis Young, of the U.S. Forest Service; William "Bud" Moore; Susan Lenard, of the Montana Audubon Society, and Kirwin Werner, of the Natural Heritage Program; Dave Hoerner, of Red Eagle Aviation in Kalispell, Montana; Susan Ireland, of the Kootenai Tribes of Idaho; and Matt Hunter with the Oregon Department of Fisheries.

We also thank Gary Luke and everyone at Sasquatch Books for their faith in our project.

Many thanks, also, to Lex Blood and Judith Pressmar, John and Kris Bruninga, Jane Adams and Andy Hyde, Steve Thompson and Kerrie Byrne, Bob and Inez Love, Fred de Lepper and Stormy Good, Denise Pengeroth, Bill and Laura Donavan, Wayne Mumford, and Jim Mann. Our families, as always, deserve our deepest thanks.

I would have liked to thank Michael Fairchild, who taught me backtracking and a thousand other backcountry lessons, but I lost the chance when he died of a heart attack in 1998 at age forty-three. In many ways, that shock prompted our explorations, both outside and within.

Index